MW00719189

Work It!

Pursue Your Passion

Live Your Purpose.....

NOW!

Joy Duckett Cain

DLite Press
P.O. Box 824
Yorktown Heights NY 10598-9998
http://www.dlitepress.com

The author does not guarantee and assumes no responsibility on the accuracy of any websites, links or other contacts contained in this book.

Work It! Pursue Your Passion, Live Your Purpose Now

PRINTING HISTORY
DLite Press/ April 2018
Cover design and digital illustration
By Robin Hoffmann

ISBN: 978-1-937143-45-9
Printed in the United States of America

ACKNOWLEDGEMENTS

First of all, I want to thank God for the many blessings that You've most graciously bestowed upon me. Although undeserving, I am humbled and deeply appreciative.

Thank you to Jasper, the most nagging /pain-in-the butt/ supportive spouse in the world. I know that it was all done with love, and this book wouldn't have existed without you.

A big shout out to my editors, Alice Jones Nelson and Dina Bentacourt, for taming me when I wanted to get a little too rowdy and "out there." Every writer needs a good editor and I was fortunate enough to have two. Thank you to Pat Hodge for your artistic help on an earlier version of this book and to Robin Hoffman for this version's wonderful cover design. Also, thank you, Marie Brown, for your time and your counsel. I deeply appreciated your input.

Thank you to Olive Peart, Heather Smith and Paul Smith for not rolling your eyes when I said that I was going to publish this book. Yes, I'd been saying that for years. And now it's done.

Thank you to my family and friends who, whether or not you were mentioned in this book, contributed something to my spirit and, consequently, to the spirit of the book. Partial roll call: My parents, Gloria and Wesley Duckett; my kids, Angela, Jelani, and Jasmine; Neal, Annette, Barry, Lisa, Marie-Elena, Cathy...... If I left out your name, please charge it to my head and not to my heart.

And finally, thank *you* for taking the time to read this book.

TABLE OF CONTENTS

Work It!

Pursue Your Passion
Live Your Purpose…..
NOW!

Joy Duckett Cain

INTRODUCTION

The day I was told I would not get a job that had been all but promised to me is the day that my foggy career path became crystal clear.

You see, sometimes it takes a denial to leapfrog you to your destiny.

Here's what happened.

For decades, I'd worked in magazines as a reporter and writer, ultimately rising to the rank of a senior editor at a major national magazine. At that time my kids were in elementary and middle school and basically, after a while, I got burned out. Tired of the commute and the office politics, annoyed at missing PTA meetings and forever rushing to make it to school concerts, I asked for, and received, a contract from the magazine to write from home. This would, I reasoned, also give me time to concentrate on one of the books floating around in my head. For a year, all was suburban bliss. Until it wasn't.

My contract with the magazine wasn't renewed and I was forced to go the freelance route. But I'll admit it: After years of being handed assignments and having stories dropped in my lap, I had become lazy. I wasn't hungry. I didn't hustle as much as I could have or should have and, as a result, my output suffered. The calls for assignments slowed down. But I wasn't sweating it. I was doing the Mommy thing and still living the American dream because, after all, my husband had a good-paying job. Until he didn't.

Caught in the economic recession, my husband lost his job as a school administrator. Suddenly, the part-time receptionist job I'd latched on to for chump change and gas money took on new importance. The oil bill had to be paid. The car note needed to be met. I dug in and freelanced a little more aggressively and I went where the dollar led…. including babysitting my friend's twin boys for half a year. Writing took a back seat. Every penny counted. And one year as a receptionist turned into two years, which turned into three years, which turned into…

Five years later, the receptionist job had become a drag. Not only was the job routine, tedious, and often intellectually numbing (qualities which, I might add, seemed appealing when I first took the gig), but getting up at 4 am to get to the job was beginning to get on my last nerve. I was looking for an out, any out, and I was also looking for more money. When an office manager's position opened up at the company I worked for, I thought I'd found both and applied for the job. On my third round of interviews, with the general manager, many nice things were said and it was obliquely hinted that I stood in very good stead to get the position. After nearly 50 interviewees, only myself and one other woman remained as candidates.

Neither one of us got the job.

I was hurt. When I asked what happened, I heard a lot of gobbledy-gook from management. They needed to tweak the position more. I didn't have office management experience. They wanted to open up the position to other candidates. Yada, yada, yada.

Yes, for a day or two the rejection hurt like hell. On the real, maybe it hurt longer than that. But eventually I saw it as the blessing that it was. If God had wanted me to get that job, I would have gotten it. So clearly, that was not where I was destined to be. Clearly, there were other things that I needed to do with my life. Clearly, it was time for me to start doing it.

You see, sometimes it takes a denial to leapfrog you to your destiny.

Hence, this book.

I've always loved words and thoughts that motivate, that help transmit you from one level to the next. When my husband and my oldest daughter both lost their jobs in the same year, I wanted to write something encouraging to help them in their job searches so I began putting little essays together. But I quickly realized that the unemployed aren't the only ones that need to be uplifted—the underemployed, like myself, could also use some encouragement. Finally, even those who may be doing what God called them to do…. sometimes, they too, need a little inspiration. And inspiration without information is fluff. So I began reading advice from people who knew the nuts and bolts of different aspects of how to get a job—and I pulled the best of what they had to say. Ultimately, I wanted to have something for all of us who are Working It—the unemployed, the underemployed, and the uninspired—and provide a little something that would resonate in our souls.

This is the result.

Many years ago, long before she became a household name, I interviewed a wise woman named Iyanla Vanzant at her Maryland home. We had a wonderful conversation, and as I parted, she gave me two books…. one of which she inscribed with words that have since become ingrained in my heart. She wrote simply: "A delay is not a denial. Have faith."

And so I say those words to you.

You may be unemployed right now, and the bills are piling up.

Have faith.

You may be underemployed right now, and your confidence is at an all-time low.

Have faith.

You may be blessed with a job that you like, but, for whatever reason, your enthusiasm lingers somewhere below sea level.

Have faith.

This moment in time is but a slice of your life, not life itself. And whatever you're going through in your work whirl today will look totally different tomorrow. Keep walking the walk. Trust. Keep working it. Believe. Remember that a delay is not a denial. Have faith.

Dig deep inside, and dare to do you.

God bless!

HOW TO READ THIS BOOK

Preferably one word at a time....

Ba-dah-bah!

But seriously, the **shaded** pages with borders feature inspirational stories; each item begins with a quote and ends with an affirmation.

The **non-shaded** pages contain advice, usually from experts in specific fields; each item has practical tips that you can use right away.

Jump around, skip pages, read in sequence—whatever your heart desires.

It's time to Work It!

Know-Nothing Naysayers

My hope for my children must be that they respond to the still, small voice of God in their own hearts.   --Andrew Young

Question: How much do the people who doubt you, who question you, who are criticizing you, really know what's in your heart? How much do they know about your potential or the fire you have in your soul? Can they fathom the depths of your yearning, of your desire to make a way out of no way? When you get down to it--how much do critics really know at all?

The answer is this: Not much.

Critics offer their opinion. Sometimes that opinion is valid, but more often than not, that opinion isn't worth the paper it's written on or the oxygen that is used to spout it. To be blunt, critics' opinions are sometimes worth doodley squat. And eventually, when the truth comes to light, the harshest critics are often shown to be the know-nothings they really are. Listen to the words of some naysayers; take note of the people they were criticizing.

"Too stupid to learn anything." (Thomas Edison)

"Possesses minimal football knowledge and lacks motivation." (Vince Lombardi)

"Can't act. Can't sing. Slightly bald. Can dance a little." (Fred Astaire)

"Too emotionally invested," and "unfit for TV" (Oprah Winfrey)

"Lacks imagination and has no good ideas." (Walt Disney)

"Why don't you stop wasting people's time and go out and become a dishwasher or something?" (Sidney Poitier)

"Not tall enough, not pretty enough, not smart enough" (Reese Witherspoon)

"You ain't going nowhere, son. You ought to be driving a truck." (Elvis Presley)

"You can't get into film. You're not pretty enough. You're not good enough." (Sally Field)

"I have an idiot for a son." (father of Rodin, the sculptor who created The Thinker)

"You sound like a goat." (music teacher to Shakira)

"The concept is interesting and well-formed, but in order to earn better than a 'C,' the idea must be feasible." (Yale University professor's response to Fred Smith's paper proposing reliable overnight delivery service. Smith went on to found Federal Express)

"Nobody wants to read a book of little short stories."

(Publisher to authors of the *Chicken Soup for the Soul* books)

Today I will listen to my heart, not the hyperbole.

The Power of Choice

Personal mastery teaches us to choose. Choosing is a courageous act: picking the results and actions, which you will make into your destiny.   -- Peter Senge

Regardless of your situation, regardless of how hemmed in you feel or how dire your straits appear to be, remember this: You still have a choice. And because you have a choice, you still have some level of control over your life. Don't believe me? Your choices are everywhere. To wit:

Should you have pizza or hamburgers for dinner? It's a choice.

Should you wear the blue jeans or the black slacks today? It's a choice.

OK: which bill gets paid this month—the light bill or the gas bill? It's a choice.

And should you latch on to that less desirable job or hold out for a better one? Once again, it's a choice.

Even when unemployment is a reality and there are no job prospects on the immediate horizon, decisions have to be made. Do you stay where you are or move somewhere else? Do you increase your skill set? Or do you reshuffle the deck entirely and embark in a totally new direction? You're the one with the answer.

Life happens. There are countless roads to take, countless decisions to make.

So the question is this: What will you choose to do?

Today I will take a fresh look at the choices in my world.

The Big "I"

The calvary ain't coming. You've got to do this yourself.

--Bettye Jean Triplett

Inspiration is as individual as each one of us. Yet its importance can't be underestimated; it is what makes you smile, what turns toil into pleasure (and hopefully treasure), what makes work worthwhile. So the question is this: What catches your eye? What causes your heart to skip a beat? What moves you enough to want to make a move?

In short: what's your inspiration?

For Chris Gardner, it was a car.

By now, his story is well known. Gardner joined the Navy after high school, and after his discharge, worked as a medical supply salesman earning $16,000 a year. One day, while loading his car, Gardner spied a red Ferrari that literally took his breath away. Gardner immediately fell in love with the car, and all that the car represented: Wealth. Class. Security.

Gardner's childhood had been anything but secure; he never knew his father and lived with his mother, Bettye, when he wasn't in foster homes. Poverty, domestic violence, sexual abuse, alcoholism, family illiteracy—that's what Gardner knew as a child.

And now, staring him in the face was the sleek, beautiful, mechanical marvel. Possibility. Totally inspired, Gardner had only two questions for the Ferrari's owner: What did he do for a living, and how could Gardner go about doing it?

Turns out that the Ferrari owner was a stockbroker. When he told Gardner that he made over $80,000 a month, Gardner, the high school graduate with no experience, no connections, and no real knowledge even of what a stockbroker did—decided that he, too, would become a stockbroker. No ifs, ands, or buts about it. His mother's words, quoted at the top of this entry, reverberated inside his soul. He had to find a way to make it happen. And he did.

Inspiration can do that to you.

Gardner's journey from medical supply salesman to stockbroker to the millionaire owner of a brokerage firm took precarious twists and turns, including divorce and homelessness, and was memorialized in the 2006 film *The Pursuit of Happyness*, starring Will Smith. But having a dream, having an inspiration, is just part of the picture.

"Ain't nobody got to dig [your dream] but you," Gardner says. "Not everybody is going to be able to see you doing what it is you are saying you want to do. You've got to be committed to it, and you've got to have a plan. Hope is not a plan. It's OK to dream, but you've got to act on it.

"What's your plan? What are the steps? Your plan has got to have something I call the C5 Complex. Your plan has got to be clear, concise and compelling, and you've got to be committed and consistent. But again," Gardner says, "ain't nobody got to see it but you."

Today, I will take flight on the wings of my inspiration.

Soul Control

But the fruit of the Spirit is love, joy, peace, patience, kindness, goodness, faithfulness, gentleness and self-control.

--Galatians 5:22-23

It's not about the situation you find yourself in; it's about the mindset you bring to that situation. You may not be able to control the stock market, the value of your home or your job situation, but you can control your attitude. And in turn, your attitude controls your disposition. So:

Is spewing hate better than showing love?

Is being glum better than jumping for joy?

Is contributing to conflict better than promoting peace?

Is exhibiting impatience better than practicing patience?

Is being mean-spirited better than being kind?

Is harboring evil better than generating goodness?

Is cheating better than faithfulness?

Is harshness better than gentleness?

Is being undisciplined better than exhibiting self-control?

Today, I will monitor the type of fruit I am bearing.

Get a Grip

Desire is half of life, indifference is half of death.

--Kahlil Gibran

It's hard to be up when you have a job only seems to bring you down. Maybe the job isn't in your field or it isn't challenging or your co-workers aren't supportive—whatever the reason, you drag yourself into each workday going through the motions without much positive emotion. Whether deep down you hate your job or whether you're merely indifferent about it, the drill is pretty much the same. You show up, punch in, do the damn thing, take a break, punch out and go home-- only to start the process all over the next day. It's a schizophrenic situation. On the one hand you're happy that at least you're picking up a piece of a paycheck, but on the other hand that paycheck comes at a hefty price. How do you spell an unsatisfying work experience?

Try G-R-I-N-D.

'Cause on the real, not every job is sunshine and bliss. Some jobs are thankless, menial, boring, low-paying, perhaps even dangerous affairs—but these jobs need to be done nonetheless. And for whatever reason, right now you're one of the people doing them. Sometimes, as Marvin Gaye used to say, it makes you want to holler…and if that's what you need to do go right ahead. But when you're finished hollering, move on, because nobody's really listening to you kvetch, anyway. Or, if you're not hollering, you may be sleepwalking through your gig. Either way, you've no desire to be where you are. The whole thing sucks. Maybe… maybe not. But consider stepping away from your pity party long enough to acknowledge the following:

You are of relatively sound mind and body; many people aren't. Be grateful.

You have a job; many people don't. Be grateful.

You can spend today being angry and disconnected or you can spend today being joyous and connected; either way, this day is going to be spent and it's not coming back. You've only got but so much time on this earth; you decide how to spend it. And while you're spending it, be grateful.

Nothing lasts forever, even if it seems otherwise. You've been on your job a lot longer than you ever dreamed you'd be, but you know what? That's all right. Because the only thing constant is change. And, cliché as it may sound, everything must change, even this Godforsaken situation that you are currently in. Take heart in that. And while you're at it, sit up a little straighter. Smile a little more. Be a little bit more approachable. What's worse than being in a dead-end job? Living a dead-end life. So put a little pep in your step, a little glide in your stride. Look up. Hold on. Better days are coming. But until they get here, make the most of this part of the journey.

Today, I will make the best of my current situation.

THE INNER GAME

Discovering what floats your boat

Know Thyself, Part 1

You can't be happy until you know what makes you happy.

This is as true in your work life as it is in your personal life, so clearly, it's important to know what floats your boat. This can only be accomplished through introspection. "Every job-seeker needs to take the time to step way from the day-to-day grind of work and spend quality time reflecting on [his] career and developing some plans for the future," observes Randall Hansen, Ph.D., author, educator, and founder of the career development website Quintessential Careers. Along those lines, Dr. Hansen suggests that the first step is that you analyze the following:

Your current/future lifestyle. Are you happy with your current lifestyle? Identify the key characteristics of your ideal lifestyle. Does your current career path allow you the lifestyle you seek?

Your likes/dislikes. Says Dr. Hansen: "What kinds of activities -- both at work and at play -- do you enjoy? What kind of activities do you avoid? Make a list of both types of activities. Now take a close look at your current job and career path in terms of your list of likes and dislikes. Does your current job have more likes or dislikes?"

Your passions. Develop a list of times you felt most passionate, energetic, engaged. How many of these times occur while you are at work?

Your strengths and weaknesses. "Step back and look at yourself from an employer's perspective," Dr. Hansen advises. "What are your strengths? What are your weaknesses? Think in terms of work experience, education/training, skill development, talents and abilities, technical knowledge, and personal characteristics."

Your definition of success. What does success look like to you? Is it: wealth, power, control, contentment? Figure out what matters most to you so that you won't waste time pursuing what doesn't.

Your personality. Extrovert or introvert? Thinker or doer? Are you someone who likes sitting behind a desk or someone who enjoys being on the move? Take a self-assessment quiz, like the ones found at http://www.quintcareers.com/career_assessment.htmlon to get a more precise picture of where you stand.

Your dream job. "Remember those papers you had to write as a kid about what you wanted to be when you grew up? Take the time to revert back to those idyllic times and brainstorm about your current dream job; be sure not to let any negative thoughts cloud your thinking. Look for ideas internally, but also make the effort to explore/research other careers/occupations that interest you," Dr. Hansen says.

Your current situation. Before you can plan to take your career somewhere else, you need to know where you are.

Becoming More Resilient

Here's the thing: If you don't like your current job situation—be it unemployment, underemployment or feeling uninspired—you've got to change it. Even Stevie Wonder can see that. But beyond the enduring question of HOW to change your situation is this: Do you have what it takes, deep inside, to MAKE a change?

Or, to put it another way—Are you resilient enough?

Isn't it incredible how one person can stub his toe and make it seem like the end of the world —while another person can have an arm amputated, stave off cancer, and bury a beloved pet— all within the same month—yet still go through each day with a smile on her face? Or how one person can lose a job and settle into a deep, seemingly unending funk while another person can lose the same job and manage to bounce back bigger and better than ever? Again, it comes down to resiliency. And while genetics plays role in how resilient each of us is, the good news is that resiliency can all be taught. Joan Borysenko, Ph.D., author of *It's Not the End of the World: Developing Resilience in Times of Change*, offers these insights.

Self-awareness is key. The first step towards resiliency is determining whether or not you are a resilient thinker. Seems kind of basic, doesn't it…but only you can make that call. Are you stuck in woe-is-me mode or are you actively looking for a way around the situation? Get real with yourself and assess where you stand on the resiliency scale.

Humor is key. "It lets you get out of your ego, out of your head, you're into the moment and you can experience joy," Dr. Borysenko says.

Mindfulness is key. Right-brained skills that allow you to see something bigger and to improvise are important. Dr. Borysenko says that in the early stages of an economic downturn, one family that owned a restaurant supply business realized that people weren't eating out as often as before. This meant that the restaurants that the family did business with probably wouldn't be faring too well…which would eventually trickle down to them— kind of a knee bone is connected to the shin bone scenario. Instead of waiting to see if the bottom would fall out, the family brainstormed and came up with an alternative plan of action BEFORE the bottom fell out. Research shows that people who have good improvisational skills are resilient.

Facing facts is very key. "It actually turns out that optimists are not resilient because they think that life is going to come and support them. Pessimists are not resilient for obvious reasons—you're negative, you can't see opportunity. However realists are the ones who really are resilient," Dr. Borysenko says.

Know Thyself, Part 2

Have you ever accepted a job or a position that you thought that you "should" accept— only to discover that the new job made you more miserable than ever before? Or perhaps you've changed careers—only to realize that your new line of work is boring you to tears? Newsflash: Just because you made a move doesn't mean that you made a move in the right direction. British-based career coach Cherry Douglas is a witness to that.

"I am a qualified careers professional," she says. "My job is to help people make the best they can of their working lives. And yet somehow I had got myself stuck on a career hamster wheel that felt a bit like death warmed up. Well, I had fallen into a familiar trap. I had been working at the same level as a career consultant for quite while and I needed a change. So I decided I should make the move to a management role." The role that she applied for and accepted had the fancy title of Deputy Director— which came with a bunch of new challenges that Douglas eventually realized didn't interest her in the least. She says that she wasn't interested in playing institutional politics or petty power games; she missed working directly with her clients. "Looking back, I can see how my role as a manager conflicted with many of my most deeply held values. It just didn't feel like me. No wonder I wasn't happy!" Douglas ultimately quit her management job and hung up her own shingle; today she offers coaching to those at a career crossroads.

And you? To find out what it takes, workwise, to make you happy, one fundamental question must first be answered: Who are you? Are you someone who learns best through doing or talking, or are you someone who learns best if you have time to think and reflect? Are you more comfortable with concrete ideas or abstract ideas? Is it your style to be honest and direct, or are you more comfortable being tactful and diplomatic? Do you get more enjoyment out of completing projects or more enjoyment out of starting projects? All these questions, and many more, are found on a simple personality assessment, which Douglas offers free of charge, on her website: http://www.how-to-change-careers.com/career-change-test.html In addition to understanding your personality type, identifying your values, skills and work motivators goes a long way towards determining what type of job is—or isn't—right for you. The How to Change Careers website will help you with these. "I am pleased to be able to say that I love my working life these days," Douglas says. "My passion is helping people to recognize when their careers are just not working for them and then supporting them as they find the courage to make the changes they need to have a more inspired working life."

How to "Grow" Your Career

In his book *The 15 Invaluable Laws of Growth*, John Maxwell shares a riddle his father used to tell him. "Five frogs are sitting on a log. Four decide to jump off. How many are left?"

"The first time he asked me," Maxwell said, "I answered one."

"No," [his dad] responded. "Five. Why? Because there is difference between deciding and doing."

Procrastinators either decide to do nothing or take forever to do a little bit of something; neither is a particularly sound strategy, especially in the work world. Like the song says, everything must change. It will change with you or without you. So the question becomes do you want to be an agent of change or a victim of change? Most of the changes procrastinators need to make are of a personal nature, but they can have a big impact on our employment picture. It's about growth. In his book, Maxwell talks about accidental growth versus intentional growth; see which side of the ledger you stack up on. Oh, and fellow procrastinators, here's a hint: One side of the ledger is definitely better to be on than the other side!

Accidental Growth	Intentional Growth
Plans to Start Tomorrow	Insists on Starting Today
Waits for Growth to Come	Takes Complete Responsibility to Grow
Learns Only from Mistakes	Often Learns Before Mistakes
Depends on Good Luck	Relies on Hard Work
Quits Early and Often	Perseveres Long and Hard
Falls into Bad Habits	Fights for Good Habits
Talks Big	Follows Through
Plays it Safe	Takes Risks
Thinks Like a Victim	Thinks like a Learner
Relies on Talent	Relies on Character
Stops Learning After Graduation	Never Stops Growing

Securing Your Financial Future

If you work at a job that you like, but don't love—chances are that you're there for the paycheck. This is not a bad thing; it's just not something that you can count on. Job security (as anyone who experienced the recessions of 2008 or 2009 can tell you) has gone the way of the gold watch.

So what are you to do? Prepare.

"Job security as we know it is dead," says financial expert William Cowie, "There still will be jobs, but they will be harder to come by and increasingly less secure. Getting and keeping these jobs will require thinking farther ahead than before. As they say in skeet shooting: don't aim where the clay pigeon is; aim where it's headed." In order to predict where the jobs are heading, Cowie offers these six suggestions.

Restate Your Goal. Simply put, your real goal is not job security, its income security. "There's a difference, and it's not just semantics. Job security focuses on "them," the job provider. Income security focuses on you." Cowie says. "You can't control them, but you can control you—and what you do. That's why you're restating your goal in terms you can actually control."

Evaluate. Take a step back and evaluate how secure your employer is; look at your paycheck provider through the eyes of customers and competitors. Read about what the press says about your employer. Cowie points out that if you worked for Circuit City a few years ago, there had been ample warning to find other opportunities before they laid off all their people. "You may love the people and the company you're with, but if top management is messing up or customers are staying away, it's better to leave first than last," Cowie says.

Become known. Use the N word—networking—at every opportunity. Become active in trade groups and on industry blogs, attend conventions and volunteer to help the movers and shakers in your field of influence. Go to picnics and social events, and make sure you are known by your boss's boss and others in your organization. It doesn't hurt to also be known by those in competing organizations and by the people who buy from your employer. "Ultimately," Cowie says, "Who you're known by is probably more important to your income security than what you know."

Become valuable. Here's the sweet spot: The intersection between what you enjoy doing most and what paying customers want. Take ownership of that sweet spot by becoming better and better at what you do; focus on your niche and grow in it. Create value. And the more valuable you become, the more income security you'll have.

Scout. "Even though you might be happy where you're at, start scouting out alternative opportunities. You don't need to take any, but it's good to know what's available where and to talk to others so you'll be ready when you do want another opportunity," Cowie says. "Also look for emerging technologies, which can spur entire new industries. The key point is to keep your head on a swivel. The first people to jump on to something new end up being the leaders."

Slash. Get your side hustle going, Cowie advises, adding that these days most entrepreneurs use the web as their storefront. "If you're going to use the web, invest a little in doing your marketing right," Cowie says. The key is to get started, even if you start small. The side hustle in your back pocket takes on new importance should your job situation become tenuous.

Ya Gotta Believe

Your belief determines your action and your action determines your results, but first you have to believe.　　--Mark Victor Hansen

Everybody believes something. The Mayans believed that the world would end in 2012. Europeans once believed that the world was flat. Only 50 years ago, some believed that man would never walk on the moon. Wrong, wrong, and wrong. Just because you believe something doesn't make it true.

Yet what you believe is powerful. Medical lore is rife with instances where one group is given a medical treatment while another group is given a placebo (or fake treatment) --but both groups showed improvement. Why? Because sometimes the power isn't really in the medicine, it is in our belief of what the medicine can do. Sometimes, it truly comes down to mind over matter. And sometimes, the matter is something you can control.

A king and a wise man were in a room. The king wanted to prove that the wise man wasn't so smart, so the king hid a small bird in the palm of his hand. He asked the wise man to tell him if the bird was dead or alive.

The wise man knew that the king was setting him up, and that if he said that the bird was alive, the king would crush it to death.

Conversely, if the wise man said that the bird was dead, the king would open his hand and let the bird fly free. After pondering a moment, the wise man responded: "Dead or alive? It's in your hands."

So what do you believe? And what can you control? Do you believe that you will never have a job as good as the one you had before? Do you believe that you're destined to lose your car your home, your savings…everything that you have? Do you believe that you're destined to lay down and die? Or do you believe that there is a way…. that there is something you can do. A phone call you can make, a person you can reach out to. Do you believe that your future is controlled by the capricious winds of Wall Street or of government or whatever else is out there? Or do you believe that you have a say in the matter of your life? Do you believe that you can do something, right here, right now, to make a difference? What is it, exactly, that you believe? And what are you willing to act on?

The action steps that I take today are in my hands.

Of Failure and Faith

You gain strength, experience and confidence by every experience where you really stop to look fear in the face. You must do the thing you cannot do.   --Eleanor Roosevelt

The beginning: He was born in an abandoned building on a floor. He was adopted. He was labeled educable mentally retarded. He failed twice in school. He didn't have college training. He never worked for a major corporation.

"To believe that I had something of value to say—that someone would want to listen to me," he says--that was the hardest thing in the world for him to do.

The middle: He started listening to motivational speakers like Zig Zigler, Robert Schuller, Dr. Norman Vincent Peale, Jim Roan. And he began getting pumped up about his possibilities...only to find that he inevitably started talking himself out of whatever euphoria he'd been experiencing.

"Most people fail in life not because they aim too high and miss, but most people fail in life because they did just like I did for so many years—they aimed too low and hit," he says. "They didn't believe in themselves."

Fortunately, this was not the end. Meet Les Brown. He used determination, persistence and belief in his abilities to take him from being a sanitation worker to becoming a broadcast station manager, a political commentator, and a multi-term state representative in Ohio.

But Brown is best known as one of the world's top motivational speakers, as he has been for the last three decades. Toastmasters International voted Brown one of the Top Five Outstanding Speakers Worldwide, and hundreds of thousands have watched his YouTube videos. Tens of thousands interact with Brown regularly on Facebook. Here's what he has to say about failure and faith; it bears repeating whether you're in the beginning, the middle or towards the end of your journey.

"A lot of people, because of failure, they stop believing," says Brown. "Let me share something with you--you will fail your way to success. Eight out of 10 millionaires have been financially bankrupt. It doesn't matter how many times you fail. It doesn't matter how many times people tell you [that] you can't do it. It doesn't matter if you don't have a dime in the bank. You will fail your way to success.

"Let me tell you when it's really tough to have faith. When you lose your job. When you lose your retirement. When you go to the doctor and they look at you and say you have cancer... that's when it's tough to have faith.

"And that's when you need to call on your faith when you need to believe in yourself and judge not according to appearances. It's possible, I can make it. It's possible, I can get through this. It's possible, I'm not going to allow this to get the best of me.

"Every day, it's a selling job on YOU. I can do this. I can make this happen. No matter how bad it is, or how bad it gets...I'm going to make it. It's possible-- yes, your dream is possible. Say that to yourself every day. Feed your faith, and your doubts will starve to death. There's nothing as powerful as a made up mind."

Today I will put my doubts on a diet.

Focus on The Now

Do not dwell in the past, do not dream of the future, concentrate the mind on the present moment.   --Buddha

The temptation is always to look elsewhere.

You want to look to the past because that is where the good times were.

You want to look to the future because that is hopefully where the better times will be.

You want to look up, down, right, left, criss-cross, sideways--anywhere, everywhere, but here. Because for whatever the reason, here is not where you want to be. Here is not a cool place, it's not a comfortable place, it's not what you dreamed of or desired for your life. But the reality is that here is where you are. And your desire to avoid where you are changes nothing. You are still here--dealing with a lousy job, searching for any job, coping with a lackluster attitude.

And Buddha said to concentrate on that?

Yes…and no.

Don't concentrate on the negatives of your situation; instead, concentrate on what you can do, right now, to get the most of this day. Should you network and update your resume (again!)? Sure. Fill out another job application and investigate updating your skill set? Absolutely. But while those actions may help you down the road, they may not make your present moment much better.

Because the present moment isn't about what you do, it is about who you are. And we are never more in the present moment than when we are enjoying life.

So enjoy. Despite everything you're going through, take a little time to enjoy yourself. Listen to your favorite song. Walk through a nearby park. Maybe even do something really revolutionary: Smile. Chances are, after you've done this you'll find that the atmosphere around you has changed even if your situation hasn't. And it's in that change of atmosphere, in that elevated attitude, that the present moment is most abundantly enjoyed and lived.

Today I will fully experience my present moments.

Keep It Moving

Success seems to be connected with action. Successful people keep moving. They make mistakes, but they don't quit. --Conrad Hilton

It's easy to get stuck in a dead end job because, hey, at least it's a job. All around you are friends and family members who aren't working, who haven't worked in a while, and who would kill--in theory, anyway-- to be in your shoes. So you stay in that job. Day after day. Month after month. Year after year.

It's a well-known fact that the best time to search for a job is when you already have one. The catch is that sometimes having a job--particularly a dead-end, mind-numbing, demoralizing job--leaves you feeling so drained and dispirited that you can't seem to summon up the energy to look elsewhere. And so there you are... day after day, month after month, year after year.

Is that really what you want?

Or maybe you have applied for other jobs. You may have gotten one, two, ten good leads. Or perhaps you've had three, four, twelve promising interviews.

There was a time when your hopes soared as high as the stratosphere, only to come crashing down after someone else landed your gig. Now here you are... day after day, month after month, year after year. Poor, poor, you!

Is that truly the best you can do?

Whether you're too beat down to look for other jobs or you're too beat down from having lost other jobs, the mantra is the same: Get up, shake it off and get moving! By now it should be clear that the fantastic, perfect job of your dreams isn't going to mosey into your present workplace and beg you to fly away with it. You're going to have to get up off of your butt and hunt it down. It's going to take some sweat, some movement, some effort on your part, to change your current situation. But trite as it may sound, there's nothing to it but to do it. Again and again and again. Take a little bitty baby step and see where it leads. Scour the classifieds. Act! Phone a friend. Move! Get LinkedIn to an old colleague. Dare! Your career is like a loaf of bread: The longer you sit around in your current situation, the staler it gets. So make like a ball and bounce. Make like a river and flow. And if things don't go your way prospect-wise or job-wise this week, try something slightly different next week. The bottom line is this: Keep it moving and don't quit. Your ultimate success--and happiness--may be just one action away.

Today I will do something to propel my destiny forward.

LOOKING FOR WORK

The search for that perfect job

Find A Job Faster By Being Organized

A cartoon on Pinterest features Maxine, an older, somewhat crotchety-looking woman, who opines the following: "I find it helps to organize chores into categories: Things I won't do now; Things I won't do later; Things I'll never do."

That's good for a chuckle, but the truth underlying that joke is real. And when it comes to embarking on a job search, not being organized can be downright disastrous.

"As simple as it may sound, the real key to finding a job faster is being organized," says Cezary Pietrzak, founder of Cezary & Co., a marketing and mobile consultancy for startups. "On a high level, staying organized means having a plan of action and executing it in an organized manner. More specifically, it's a set of behaviors that allow you to manage your time effectively and focus your efforts on the highest-value tasks." To increase your chances of finding a new job, Pietrzak suggests following these six principles:

- Set Goals. Duh… not exactly rocket science, right? Right… but your goals need to be specific; just "getting a job" is way too broad. "You need to be more specific about interim goals, add time constraints to make them real, and write them down to make yourself accountable," Pietrzak says. "What tasks do you want to accomplish by the end of the first month? How many interviews do you expect to have by the end of three? How many new opportunities can you find through warm introductions?" This is important because it gives you something to work towards through each step of the process.

- Prioritize your tasks. Think about the most important thing you need to start your job search; determine how many hours a day you can realistically spend looking; think twice about going to another networking event or meeting with companies you don't care about. Time is your most valuable commodity, so use it wisely.

- Eliminate Distractions. Pietrzak advises you to a) find a proper, dedicated workspace for your job search b) unless absolutely necessary, turn off your mobile phone, social networks, app notifications, etc. c) avoid non-essential tasks (like making plans for the weekend or running personal errands) until you've done your search or met your goals for the day.

- Use the Right Tools. Align yourself with the appropriate job boards; keep track of your progress through apps like Rake (which lets you streamline all of your job search activity in one place); keep your schedule organized in an easy-to-navigate calendar program like Google Calendar;

use social media dashboards like HootSuite to identify and monitor important professional connections.

- Create a routine. Although the job market is unpredictable, your routine needn't—and shouldn't—be. Says Pietrzak: "Start by dividing each day into manageable chunks. Check emails and scan social networks when you wake up, send follow-up notes and make phone calls in the morning, research new opportunities during lunch time, take coffees and interviews in the afternoon, and reserve evenings for networking events. Then, create routines for each individual job. Follow up with two emails and one phone call after submitting an application, and send a thank you note one day after an interview. Lastly, get into the habit of asking people for help, whether it's your friends or new professional contacts. Focus on being consistent and following through with your plan, rather than stressing out about the details of your approach."

- Stay optimistic. Yes, that is easier said than done, but it is not impossible—even if you're unemployed. In fact, it is especially if you're unemployed that optimism is needed the most. "One of the marquee traits of organized people is optimism in achieving their goal, no matter how big or challenging. Rather than complaining, they seek support from others around them. They celebrate small victories and reward themselves for achieving milestones. And they remove themselves from negative environments, ignoring things they cannot control," Pietrzak concludes. "It's easy to get wrapped up in the day-to-day frustrations of the job search, but try to remember the end goal: a challenging new job, a big career move, and one step closer to achieving your professional potential."

Targeted Job Hunting

A targeted job hunt is—as the term implies—systematic and focused. "When you do targeted research, generally you concentrate on an industry or a geographic preference," notes David E. Perry, a.k.a. The Rogue Recruiter. Perry says that ways to do this with regards to a job hunt include:

Doing an advanced Google search. After clicking on the advanced tag, enter your industry and/or location of choice. You can also set time parameters; for instance you can limit your search to all jobs listed within the last day, week or month. Similarly, you can narrow your search down to a particular company.

Mining your target company's website. Once you know which companies you'd like to work for, Perry advises that you go to their website and find out the names of the people who can actually hire you. "Those people are the executives-- not the human resource people -- they can only say no (unless you're a human resources professional)," Perry says. "If you're lucky, every web site will identify their senior executives, including names, titles, phone numbers, career summaries and sometimes email and photos. Web information should be up-to-the-minute accurate, but I would call the receptionist and confirm it." If you can't find the correct contact on the website, Perry suggests going back to Google's advanced search box, typing in the company name and the title of the person you seek to find (i.e., VP Sales Marketing) where appropriate. A list of people who held that position should come up.

Using LinkedIn, Spokeo, or ZoomInfo. Once you find the name of the person one rung up the ladder from where you want to be, go back to Google. If you type their first and last name and the company name, again, where appropriate, a list of press releases and news articles in which that person is mentioned should appear. Read an article or a clip or two of theirs-- then, when you reach out to them in a letter, you'll be able to say that you read their article about such and thus, which prompted you to write. That's separating you from the pack and going the extra mile. It is also, in Perry's words, "very powerful."

Benefits of a Niche Job Board

According to a recent survey by CareerXroads, nearly 65% of all job openings are filled either internally or through referrals; people who had used job boards filled 12%. Clearly the phrase "it's not what you know, it's who you know," still has merit, but if used the right way, so do job boards. "The trick is knowing how to use them and understanding their limitations," says Paul Bernard, founder and principal of Paul Bernard & Associates, a New York-based executive coaching and management consultant firm. "It's important to realize, though, that all job boards are not created equal."

To illustrate, Bernard recommends that instead of using a behemoth job board like Monster.com, you should opt for job board aggregators instead. Aggregators gather and display listings from hundreds of online job boards, then allow you to search for a job based on your desired position and location. Indeed.com, Simplyhired.com, and Careerjet.com are examples of such aggregators. But Bernard says that there is another way to go-- through niche job boards that specialize in particular job functions or industries. (Some of Bernard's best niche board picks can be found in the Resource section at the back of this book.) "They often list positions that don't appear on some of the larger, general boards, so they can offer access to openings with smaller applicant pools," he says. "Applying for a job through a niche board can also give you a leg up over someone using a broad-based site because it identifies you as more of an industry insider."

Still, nothing beats the personal touch. At the end of the day, regardless of what job you eventually land, at some point you'll have to deal with people. So the more people, the merrier. Bernard recommends that you take a 10-20-70 approach to finding a job: spend 10 percent of your time searching online, 20 percent of your time interacting with recruiters (if appropriate), and 70 percent of your time networking in person, on the telephone, or through person-to-person online contacts (made through introductions or renewal of old acquaintances). "Rather than using job boards as a one-stop method to find work, think of them as research tools to get a sense of the skills and experience that are in demand, as well as to help you refine your search and nuance your personal pitch," Bernard says. "Then network like mad!"

Using an Advanced Job Search

Despite the appealing specificity of niche job boards, millions of job seekers still flock to the major job boards and search engines to find employment. But many hunters aren't using these sites to their best advantage. Alison Doyle, a highly-regarded expert who knows how to take advantage of all the resources available to job seekers, says that utilizing the advanced search capabilities of job boards and search engines can be a big help. "A shorter, but better matched, list will help you save job searching time," she says. "There will be fewer job listings that aren't a good fit to read through. When you apply for jobs that are as close a match as possible your chances of getting chosen for a job interview will increase."

Here are four of Doyle's tips (first reported on in balance.com) on how to use an advanced job search to your advantage.

1. Click on the advanced search option; typically it's in small font on the first page of the job site. " It will bring you to a page where you can specify criteria to refine your search by more options than the keyword and location options on the front page of the site," she says. Although sites differ in terms of categories you can search by, some of the more common options include: city; date posted;

education; experience; keywords (that you can include or exclude); industry; job function; radius (within X miles); salary; state; type of job (full time, internship, seasonal, telecommute, etc.) and zip code. "Narrowing your search criteria by the factors that are most important to you will you give you a shorter, but more relevant list of available jobs," notes Doyle.

2.   If possible, get clear on your category or type of job. On Career Builders, Doyle notes that new graduates can select the category "entry level" to generate a list of first jobs. Current college students can select the job type "internship" to get a list of options for the college years. "You can also specify the level of education appropriate for your situation," Doyle adds. "The job type function also allows you to focus on or eliminate part-time, seasonal, full-time, contract, temporary or volunteer positions, depending on the site you're using."

3.   But beware of becoming *too* specific. Say your dream job involves doing creative work in the marketing department of a specific company. You could narrow your search to just those elements, but you might come up empty. Doyle suggests that you can include many criteria at the start of your search, but be ready to remove less important factors if the list of jobs generated is too restrictive. Also

recognize that not all jobs are coded properly; search in different ways if you aren't happy with your output.

4. Finally, Doyle reminds us that search results vary from site to site. "Don't presume that you'll get the same results on Indeed as on SimplyHired, for example, even though they both list jobs from many different sources," she says. "The query factors and the code that generates the results are different depending on which site you are using. It's important to not miss out on what could be a perfect job, so try a variety of advanced search options and job sites to make sure you're getting good matches."

Searching For A New Job on the Sly, Part 1

If you've decided that you're ready to do what it takes to get on up and out of that dead-end job, congratulations! But if you need that dead-end job's paycheck until you find greener pastures, take heed. Not everyone (read: your boss) needs to know what your game plan is. In fact, others should be informed strictly on a need-to-know basis—if they can't help in some way, then they don't need to know. If you're yearning for a different place to do your earning, remember that discretion is the better part of valor. So:

Never use your current job's e-mail to contact prospective employers. Aside from the fact that your current boss probably has access to everything that is on your work computer, the fact that you aren't cautions to shows a lack of judgment. Big no no.

Never post resume details on job boards that your present employer might look at. On Monster, for example, there are ways to put in a generic company name and block out contact information and reference details. Include your job-searching e-mail address and cell phone number.

Never use your current job's office equipment. Besides the computer being monitored, often the phone calls are monitored as well—and if the wrong person picks up your line while you are away from the desk, well, you fill in the blanks. Similarly, forget about making copies of your resume or cover letter on the office copy machine; even if you don't accidentally leave telltale copies behind, other things can go wrong, i.e., for instance… can you say paper jam? This is what OfficeMax and places like that are for.

Searching For A New Job on the Sly, Part 2

The best time to look for a job is when you already have one—even if your current job is one that you don't care for or one that you are abundantly overqualified for. Even so, is it a good idea to advertise that you're looking around? Unless you have a fabulous relationship with your employer—or, conversely, if you don't give a flying fig—the answer is probably no. Still, there is a right way and a wrong way to act as you clandestinely conduct your job search. Remember to:

- Always dress the part; if you work in a jeans and T-shirt environment, showing up in a business suit is a dead giveaway. Go the Clark Kent route and change into your interview clothes somewhere else. This change of costume routine can occur more easily if you…

- Always schedule interviews to take place during your lunch hour, at the beginning or at the very end of the day. The less attention that is caused by your absenteeism, the better.

- Always network with the RIGHT people; this includes family, friends, past co-workers, even present co-workers IF THEY ARE TRUSTWORTHY. If there's a question in your mind about whether or not someone can keep his mouth closed about your job search, do yourself a favor and say nothing. Loose lips sink ships…and nip prospective job opportunities in the bud.

- Always use your time productively. While you can't job search on your work computer, you can use your cellphone or go to a place with Internet access before or after work or during lunchtime and do your searching then. Lunchtime is also a great time to return prospective employer's calls, particularly if you go to lunch a little bit early or late and can catch your prospective boss when he or she returns from lunch.

- Always remember that social media is omniscient; don't put anything on the web that you don't want your boss to find out about. You've been around the block a time or two; you know that someone doesn't have to be your friend or in your network to know what color your Kool-Aid is. Discretion, discretion, discretion!

Cover Letters and Common Courtesy

In this age of solar panels, Snapchat and the ever-present online job applications—is there room for the quaint, oh so 20th century cover letter? According to the folks at Robert Half, the world's largest staffing agency, there is. "Many job applicants assume a cover letter, or, nowadays, an introductory note submitted in an online job application system, won't matter," their website says. "It does." In fact, a well-crafted cover letter can make you stand out from the crowd in three important ways:

It highlights that you can write with clarity and introduces your communication style to your potential employer.

Coupled with a targeted resume, it shows you took the time to tailor your application for the job.

You can "go longer" in explaining how your previous responsibilities or efforts on a specific project align with what the job opening requires.

The website points out, however, that because recruiters and HR people are under time constraints, cover letters should be limited to only two or three paragraphs.

"Digital communication has changed how you address a hiring manager when contacting the person for the first time or when sending a thank-you note after an interview," the website continues. "Yet, you need to attend to each of the following points of business etiquette with just as much care today as you did a decade ago." Their advice:

Avoid the salutations "To whom it may concern" or "Dear Sir or Madam." Take the time to seek out the name of the recruiter or manager who is hiring, even if it means picking up the phone to find it.

If you make it to the interview stage, send a thank-you note promptly. A handwritten note may make you stand out, but perhaps not in the way you'd hoped. Because a snail-mail note takes longer to arrive and is more likely to be lost, it's better to email your thanks.

If you are tempted to thank by text or tweet, don't. While a speedy thanks is a good idea, using email keeps that communication on a much more professional level.

Age Ain't Nothing But A Number, Part 1

For everything there is a season,
And a time for every matter under heaven:
A time to be born, and a time to die
A time to plant, and a time to pluck up what is planted
A time to kill and a time to heal
A time to break down and a time to build up...

--Ecclesiastes 3:1-3

When is the right time to launch a business?

Is it in your 20s, when you are ambitious, energetic and probably footloose and fancy-free? Logic seems to suggest that that is a good time.

Or is it in your 30s, when you're still energetic and enthusiastic but you have a few years of experience under your belt? Logic seems to suggest that that is also a good time.

If that ship has sailed, though, perhaps when you're in your 40s is the best time to start a business. True, you may have more personal responsibilities, but time may have morphed you into a more responsible and reasoned person, conscious of risks but calculating in your approach to taking them. Surely, this is a logical time to start a new venture.

Then there's your 50s and 60s. Since we're going with logic here, let's get real: Doesn't it seem slightly illogical that someone who has spent thirty plus years in the workforce would suddenly want to start something new? Shouldn't that seasoned citizen be content in just counting the days until he or she receives that first Social Security check---if, indeed, Social Security even survives?

Well, there's logic—and then there's this: According to the Kauffman Ewing Institute, 25.8 percent of all new entrepreneurs in 2015 were between the ages of 55 and 64. Furthermore, a previous Institute study of 5,000 new start-up companies noted 48 percent had founders who were 45 years of age or older. (The years studied were 2004-2008.) But here's the real kicker: Of the start-ups that survived, a whopping 64 percent were run by entrepreneurs who were 45 and up. That report concluded, "Previous industry experience and start-up experience had less impact on firm survival prospects than did owner age." Hmmm. Perhaps it's not called the Golden Years for nothing.

Yet no one in their right mind can overlook Mark Zuckerberg, who launched Facebook when he was 20 or Jeff Bezos who started Amazon when he was 30 or Mark Pincus who created Zynga, (online games like Farmville and Cityville) when he was 41. Likewise, there's no dismissing the reams of 20, 30, and forty-something year olds who have started a multitude of successful businesses, albeit on a smaller scale.

So when it comes to launching a business, when is the best time to start?

All logic aside, it seems to be whenever your spirit urges you to do so.

Today I will explore whether my season
to start my new business is now.

For Love, Not Money

You have brains in your head. You have feet in your shoes.
You can steer yourself in any direction you choose. You're on your own.
And you know what you know. You are the guy who'll decide where to
go.   --Dr. Seuss

Consider, for a moment, the case of Alvah Curtis Roebuck.

In 1893 he and his employer, Richard Warren Sears, joined forces to launch a catalog business called Sears Roebuck and Company. The company was based in Chicago. Two years later, fearing that the nascent venture was destined to fail, Roebuck asked Sears to buy him out for about $20,000. Sears did, and the rest is history. At its peak, Sears Roebuck and Co. was estimated to have sales of $4,000 per minute. And of course, the brick and mortar Sears remains one of the nation's longest-standing retail chains.

Let's face it: Most of us would still be kicking ourselves if we allowed a deal like that to fall through our fingertips. So it's interesting to note how Roebuck responded to this change of fortune.

First, he bore no ill will. As sales soared through the stratosphere, Roebuck agreed to continue working with the company, handling the division that sold watches, jewelry, glasses, and later, motion picture machines. Eventually Roebuck started two side businesses of his own, then semi-retired to Florida. The stock market crash of 1929, however, forced him to return to Chicago. By 1933 he was back at Sears Roebuck and Company, compiling a history of the company he helped found. Soon, he was making public appearances at retail stores around the country, talking up the brand and its history. With or without ownership, the company was in Roebuck's blood and he loved being associated with it. All told, Roebuck spent 45 years in and out of the firm he helped found. Sears, on the other hand, died in 1914 at the age of 51, just over 20 years after founding the company.

So to the inevitable question--how did he feel about his own modest wealth compared to the vast fortune Richard Sears amassed--Roebuck, who died in 1948 at the age of 84, had a standard reply. "He's dead. Me? I never felt better."

Today I will remember that he who dies with the most money doesn't necessarily win.

A Matter of Perspective

Humor is just another defense against the universe.

--Mel Brooks

Dr. Bennett Neiman has worn many hats during his professional career. Teacher, owner of a multi-million dollar advertising agency, child protective agency worker, consultant—these are just some of the jobs that he's had during his long and largely fulfilling work life. Yet there have been times when Neiman's been between gigs—and he relates the following story about what happened during one of these times of unemployment.

As was his custom, every morning Neiman drove his wife to the local diner where they'd have breakfast together before he drove her to work. One day, the owner of the diner told them that the guy who usually opened the diner had taken ill and would be out for a couple of weeks; since Neiman wasn't working anyway—would he consider filling in for a while?

Neiman was told that opening the diner basically meant making coffee and selling the occasional donut or bagel until the cook and the owner arrived at around 8:00am. At that point, the owner said, Neiman would be free to leave.

Despite having a Ph.D., since Neiman really didn't have anything else going on in his life work-wise, he agreed to fill in. To his surprise, he discovered that he enjoyed it. He chatted with the customers, using his psychology skills to explore what was going on in their lives. He made coffee, served donuts. He began thinking that owning his own diner someday might not be a bad idea.

In time, the employee that Neiman had been filling in for got better and returned to his job. Neiman left and went on to run for a seat on his town's school board. Then he auditioned for, and won, a leading role in a community theater company production; the reviews were good and his face was plastered all over the pages of the local paper. Next, Neiman was asked to fill in as headmaster at a Jewish school whose leader had left midway through the school year, and he agreed to do so. Life went on. A few months later, a woman stopped Neiman on the street. "I know you!" she said. Neiman proceeded to tick off the places she might have known him from. The Jewish school? No. The local play? Nah. Perhaps she remembered when he ran for school board? Nope.

Suddenly, the woman's face lit up. "I know what it is," she exclaimed enthusiastically. "You're the guy from the diner!!!!"

Neiman smiles as he retells the story. "Whenever things are going well and I'm tempted to get a big head," he says. "I always remember that lady. It reminds me that, at the end of the day… I'm just the guy from the diner."

Today I will refuse to take myself too seriously.

Mind Games

Nothing is impossible; the word itself says, "I'm possible!"

--Audrey Hepburn

For ten years, Stephen Hopson worked a 9-5 job at a major Wall Street bank, essentially going nowhere fast. Hard as he tried, he never managed to crack the bank's glass ceiling. So Stephen did what many sensible people do: He looked for another job. Merrill Lynch was looking for stockbrokers, and the qualifications for that job seemed to fit Stephen to a tee. Enthusiastically, he applied for the position.

Stephen's first meeting was with a branch vice president. Determined not to blow the opportunity, Stephen kept his appointment with the VP, despite the fact that he had a cold and a 101-degree fever. The two talked for over three hours, and Stephen was sure he would be offered a position.

Not quite. The VP told Stephen that next he would have to meet with 12 of his top stockbrokers. Over the next five months, Stephen did so, although they didn't exactly form a cheering squad. Most of the stockbrokers told him it would be best if he played it safe and stuck with his 9-5 bank job. But Stephen was nothing if not persistent; he plowed on. He completed a 25-page marketing plan and met with the VP for a final interview. Not willing to pull the trigger and hire him outright, the VP told Stephen that he'd have to resign from his bank job, complete Merrill Lynch's three-month training program, and then pass the stockbroker exam on his first try in order to get hired. If he failed the exam by even one point, he'd be outta there. Shaken but not deterred, Stephen accepted the challenge.

He made it. Over the next four years, Stephen worked his butt off to become one of the top salespeople at his branch, building and managing multimillion dollar investment portfolios for his clients, earning a six-figure income, and garnering a spot in the prestigious Merrill Lynch Executive Club three years in a row. But by the beginning of his fifth year, Stephen realized that he was becoming spiritually bankrupt and depressed. In looking back over his life, he realized that the times he was happiest, the times he felt most alive, was when he had the opportunity to speak to others.

When he had speaking engagements, he had always been able, with humor, to connect emotionally with his audience, in some instances even transforming some lives.

So, prayerfully, Stephen decided to switch it up again. He gave up his lucrative investment-banking career to begin again, this time as a motivational speaker. The road hasn't been easy and there have been many peanut butter and jelly sandwiches along the way, but today, Stephen Hobson is happy. He is a full-time motivational speaker. He is an author (*Obstacle Illusions*) and contributing author (*Chicken Soup for the College Soul*). And in 2001 and 2003, respectively, he fulfilled a childhood dream by earning his private and commercial pilot's licenses.

Oh, there's one more thing Stephen is. Stephen Hopson is deaf.

Today, I will remind my mind that nothing is impossible.

THE OUTER GAME

Making a marvelous first impression

Perfecting Your Elevator Pitch

The phrase "elevator pitch" stems the scenario of serendipitously meeting someone important in an elevator. This person is a honcho in your field, a mover and a shaker, someone who could make your employment dreams come true in a heartbeat. What could you say about yourself, in the thirty second to minute-long span of an elevator ride, that would make an impression on that person? Could you sum up the height and depth, the wit and wisdom of who you are and what you have to offer in a sixty second sound bite? Do you have an elevator pitch? If not, now's the time to get one.

Career coach and author Nancy Collamer breaks the process of perfecting an elevator pitch into these nine parts:

1. Clarify your job target; nail down the best way to describe your field and your type of position you want. If you don't have that straight, how can you expect anyone else to?

2. Write it down; list everything you'd want a prospective employer to know about your skills and experience relevant to the job you want. Then brutally edit everything that isn't germane to your pitch. "Your goal is to interest the listener in learning more, not to tell your whole life story," Collamer explains. "So remove extraneous details that detract from your core message."

3. Format it; your pitch should answer three questions: Who are you? What do you do? What are you looking for?

4. Tailor the pitch to them, not you. The person listening to your pitch is interested in what's in it for them—so make sure that you deliver. "Using benefit-focused terminology will help convince an interviewer that you have the experience, savvy and skills to get the job done in his or her business."

5. Avoid using industry jargon; now's not the time to show off what you know—it's the time to be clear and accessible.

6. Read your pitch out loud; you don't want to come off sounding like an infomercial instead of a person.

7. Practice. Stand in front of a mirror or use the recorder on your cellphone to practice until your delivery becomes effortless. Then solicit feedback from friends to see if there are tweaks they can offer that will make it better. Finally, practice some more. And some more. You want your pitch to come as easily to you as breathing does.

8. Prepare a few variations; the way you'd pitch a former co-worker working at your desired place of employment is different than the way you'd speak to the president of that same company. Also, you need to have a 15 second pitch (for a short elevator ride) as well as a longer one. Go back

to the computer; in general, you can say about 150 words in a minute.

9. Ooze confidence. "When you give the speech, look the person in the eye, smile and deliver your message with a confident, upbeat delivery," Collamer says. "Get your pitch right and you might soon find yourself riding an actual elevator at your new job."

Handling the Interview Process

When—notice that we didn't say "if"—you land that face-to-face job interview, you'd better have more to say than just hello. Once inside that sacred interview arena, you've got to be on top of your game. "Because there are so many different questions that can be asked in a job interview, it is helpful to have some general guidelines to help you answer any job interview question," says career expert Susan P. Joyce. Since 1998, Joyce has published, edited and written for Job-Hunt.org ad she has written for WorkCoachCafe.com since 2011. Here are some of Joyce's "do's" and "don'ts" on how to successfully handle the interview process.

Job Interview "Do's"

Do listen very carefully. In your actions during a job interview, you are demonstrating your quality as an employee. Show that you will understand what you are asked to do, if hired.

Do answer the question that was asked. Repeat it back, if you want to be sure. After you have answered the question asked, you can carefully add more information to put your "spin" on the question, following the rest of the guidelines. However, this is not the time to be a politician and answer the question you wish they had asked.

Do speak honestly. This doesn't mean that you need to tell every detail that you know, but be sure that what you share is true.

Do be brief. The longer the explanation, the more troublesome it could be for you.

Do stay on topic. Resist the impulse to throw in additional "related" information. The interviewers may not see the same relevance that you feel is there, and they may think you are scattered in your thinking.

Do stay positive. Focus on being positive in your answers. Trash talking is a killer in an interview. Even if the interviewer is talking trash, resist. They could be baiting you to see if you will reveal something you shouldn't.

Do stick to the facts. Try not to offer opinions unless specifically asked for your opinion, and then, when offering your opinion, be as even-handed as you can be.

Do have your own questions ready. Demonstrate your interest, intelligence, and preparation by having good questions to ask. You'll impress the employer and you will hopefully help yourself avoid a job that isn't a good fit for you.

Do be very well prepared. So many job seekers blow their opportunity at a job by walking into the interview unprepared. That shows lack of interest as well as lack of respect to the employer.

Job Interview "Don'ts"

Don't be modest. This is not the time to avoid bragging. Describe your accomplishments and achievements that are relevant to the questions you are asked. The best way to do this is to make a list of your accomplishments and achievements. Build the list through brainstorming with family, friends, and former colleagues, going through performance reviews and other documents you have from your jobs. Before the interview, practice talking about your accomplishments and achievements out loud, hopefully to a friend or family member so you are comfortable saying them out loud.

Don't be an entertainer. You may be very witty, and you can certainly let your wit show in an interview, particularly at the end of an interview if you feel you have developed some rapport with the interviewers. But, don't focus on making them laugh – unless you are interviewing for a job as a comedian or entertainer.

Don't ask about salary or benefits in the first interview. Find out whether or not the job is a good fit before you ask about salary and benefits. Asking those questions in the first interview will often kill employer interest in you; it's a sign to them that you are only interested in the money, not the job. Yes, salary and benefits are important issues to both sides, but better discussed nearer the end of the process than the beginning.

"Other 'don'ts for interview behavior include don't answer your cellphone, don't text or email, don't dress inappropriately, and don't be late," Joyce says.

Look The Role for the Job You Want

Having great qualifications and being resume ready are only part of the job search equation; the other part is visual. You've got to make a good impression. And you've got to look the role.

Some of this is common sense; if you want to get a job as a truck driver, you don't show up at the interview in a tux. Some other common sense notions to keep in mind include:

Grooming matters. Great suit plus lousy haircut and ragged fingernails equal bad first impression.

Color matters. In general, blue or gray are safe colors to wear at an interview, as is the conventional white shirt or blouse; red, orange and yellow are no-nos.

Trendiness matters…but don't be too trendy. When in doubt, lean towards the conservative.

Accessories matter. In this case, however, less is more. Unless you're in an artistic field, excessive chains and body piercings can put the kibosh on your employment prospects before you even utter a word.

Fitting in matters… to an extent. Just because everyone in the office wears jeans doesn't give you permission to show up at your interview in jeans; wear khaki's and a casual but well-ironed shirt instead. Dress slightly up, but not so up that you make others uncomfortable.

Attitude matters. Remember that you're never fully dressed without a smile, and a genuine smile can translate into a confident persona. And confidence-- combined with the right look and the right qualifications-- is often a winning combination!

Handling the Interview Process, Part 2

In a job interview—as in life— there's a lot riding not only on what you say, but how you say it. And while this may not be grammatically correct, it is also important who you "be." Maureen Crawford Hentz, a nationally-recognized expert on recruiting and job searching, offers additional pointers on how to "be" so that you can ace your next job interview.

Be personable. Your phone interview may be the highlight of your day, but remember, to the interviewer, you may be the 16th encounter. Clearly, you need to differentiate yourself from the pack. "Don't be so stiff and formal that I can't engage with you. I like to hear you laugh during a phone interview," Hentz says. "Think about it like Halloween and trick or treating. The kid who comes to the door and is in a homemade Martian costume when everyone else is dressed as Buzz Light Year is the one you want to be. He gets extra candy and he gets talked about."

Be aware of your X factor. Being qualified for the job isn't enough; your interviewer needs to be wowed by whatever it is that makes you special. " I want to hire the dorkiest people, the people who are the most into their jobs. I want the person who reads the journals, who asks me if we will pay for professional conferences. I want to send you to a conference. I want you to ask, "Are there industry journals available? Is there a program that will help me make my skills better?" says Hentz. "It's not that I don't want you to play soccer at lunch, I do…I just want to also know that you care about the work and your own professional development."

Be inquisitive. Ask about how to grow in the job; how do people prepare for the next job. Often, this question can reveal what skills are most important to the company. Also, ask if the interviewer if there are any questions you should be asking; this gives him or her an opportunity to expound on something you may not have talked about yet.

Be generous. "One thing that I've seen candidates do occasionally really well is to refer candidates. If you know that a company is hiring for multiple positions, refer your friends—even after you've interviewed, "Hentz says. "Let me know you've sent your friends. It exudes confidence and it makes you a value-added candidate. It shows you are already working for the company before you are hired. That is really, really impressive."

Be well mannered. Sending a thank you note never goes out of style; do it. But following up by phone two or three days after your interview…can you say desperate? Chill. Companies that are worth their salt will let candidates know when a hiring decision has been made.

Creating Your Personal Brand in One Hour

Kleenex, McDonalds, Nike—most people are familiar with these famous brands. What is sometimes less familiar to folk is what a personal brand is—and why little old you—the competent accountant, English teacher, or geologist that you are—need to have a brand in the first place. Well, if you are content with where you are—perhaps you don't need a brand. But if you're looking to make a change in your life, if you're ready to move from one arena to another or from one level to the next, then creating a personal professional brand may be key. This is especially true if you want to go into business.

"All of us need to understand the importance of branding," says management guru Tom Peters. "We are CEOs of our own companies: Me Inc. To be in business today, our most important job is to be head marketer for the brand called You."

Simply put, a personal brand represents how you want to be known in the business world. It is the hook that you hang your hat on, the special something that separates you from all the other accountants, English teachers, and geologists out there. Joshua Waldman, founder of CareerEnlightenment.com and author of *Job Searching with Social Media for Dummies*, says that the following three-step exercise should help you nail your personal brand within an hour.

Step 1—Ask yourself and write down the answers to the following questions: What qualities do I have that help me do my job better than anyone else? How have previous employers remembered me? What are the three things I want someone to remember about me when they first meet me?

Step 2—Make sure your answers are consistent. Look at what you wrote down. Do the answers reflect who you are as a person? Do they solve real business challenges of the companies you've targeted? Do your resume and online profiles reflect this message? If not, make adjustments to your pitch/brand position.

Step 3—Boil it down to its essence. Once you're comfortable with the description of your brand, boil it down to a statement... something like "I'm Josie and I'm a database wizard with a passion for complexity," or "I'm Mark and I love translating business problems into on-time deliverables."

Play with your brand. Get comfortable with it. Once you're clear on who you are and what your personal brand is, you'll be that much closer to nailing the job of your dreams.

Releasing Your Personal Brand to the World

Creating a personal brand is just one piece of the puzzle. The bigger piece involves letting the rest of the world know who you are and what you are about. "Visibility creates opportunities," says personal branding expert Dan Schawbel, author of *Me 2.0* "Brand yourself for the career you want and not the job you have."

There are many ways to build a professional brand, but some you may want to look at first involve:

Getting your name out there. Make contact with some of the important people in your field by sending a message to them on their website or networking profile. If they respond, great. If they don't keep at it. At the very least, your name will be one that they recognize. And that's a start.

Getting into the mix. Attend industry events, write articles, make contacts in your field. It's the N word here: Network!

Writing your own blog. Obvious, sometimes hackneyed, but a potentially winning move. Focus on your area of expertise and use your blog as a worldwide calling card.

Building a website. Quite simply, there is no better way to show what you're about. Web-hosting services like Go Daddy and Hostgator can do it for you or break it down so that building your own website becomes a relatively painless process.

Using the web constructively. Resources that can help you build your brand more effectively include—JibberJobber (which keeps track of networking contacts), LinkedIn (ask and answer LinkedIn questions to increase your visibility), and VisualCV (a digital way to share what you've done with contacts and prospective employers).

The bottom line is that you should take promoting your personal brand seriously. "You have to be as committed to your personal brand as you are to your husband or wife," Schawbel says. Now *that's* serious!

Personal Brand No-Nos

En route to creating your personal brand, what you avoid doing is every bit as important as what you actually do. Chief among personal branding no-nos is letting your personal life seep into your professional sphere. If you can grasp that the raunchy photo of you dancing on top of that table at your cousin's birthday party is just one Google search away, well, you can also grasp that it might behoove you to carefully monitor such images.

Tim Ferris, author of *The Four-Hour Work Week,* puts it this way. "Personal branding is about managing your name — even if you don't own a business — in a world of misinformation, disinformation, and semi-permanent Google records. Going on a date? Chances are that your "blind" date has Googled your name. Going to a job interview? Ditto." Bottom line: Privacy settings exist on social media sites like Facebook for a reason; don't be afraid to use them!

As you get your personal brand together, there are a few other don'ts to keep in mind.

Don't have an unfocussed, seemingly random web presence. Take the time to decide how you want to present yourself to the world, create a plan for that presentation, and stick to it.

Don't rely too much on past achievements. What you've accomplished is all well and good, but your personal brand exists so that you can do even more!

Don't blog about something unless it is relevant to your career field. If you want to be the top financial advisor in your town, blogging about your dog isn't going to help. Unless, of course, your potential clients are of the four-legged variety.

Don't be stingy with your networks or contacts; help them whenever possible. If you want them to rub your back, you've got to rub theirs.

Don't sleep on the importance of positive feedback. Let clients, customers, and friends that you've worked with in the past put in the good word for you online; glowing testimonials are always a good thing.

Don't allow sloppiness to seep into your content; a thousand words of jibberish is still nothing but a whole lot of jibberish. Always emphasize quality over quantity.

The Basics on Business Cards

You've decided to step up and step out into your own business venture. Cool beans. You've done your research, worked out your business plan. Double cool beans. Perhaps you've even started building your website. Triple cool beans. Now it's time to work on person-to-person marketing and get your business card in place. Marketing expert Tim Tyrell-Smith says that this is where many entrepreneurs fall short.

"Everyone should have a business card, right?" Tyrell-Smith asks. "Whether you have a business, a nonprofit, a local organization or are looking for a new job, you need a way to leave people with important information. But most make big mistakes on their cards." To illustrate, Tyrell-Smith ticks off these ten business card miscues.

1. Small font size. You don't want to miss out on lots of clients or customers simply because they can't read what you have to offer. Tyrell-Smith says to show something in your projected font size to a variety of people and ask them if they can read what it says.

2. Glossy paper. "One way I can make your card more usable and memorable is to make some notes on it before I leave you," says Tyrell-Smith. " But if you have a varnish on top, you make that hard. Will your cards get a little dirty

without it? Yes. But I'd rather be able to write on your card."

3. Light font color. Again, see point #1. Your card needs to be readable. 'Nuff said.

4. Design inconsistent with website. There is value—and great brand recognition—in having a card design that integrates the look and feel of your brand. Be consistent.

5. No links to social media sites. "If you use Facebook, Twitter or YouTube to attract people to your brand, shouldn't you include links to those sites on your business card? It's a great way to encourage more fans and followers simply by letting people know how to find you," Tyrell-Smith says.

6. No email address or bad email address. This is another no-brainer; if a potential client isn't ready to talk to you right now, how can they reach you later? If you don't have a website, use your LinkedIn profile (as long as you're not too lazy on LinkedIn.) Then there's this: Tyrell-Smith tells of viewing two cards with nice logos and business names, but with Gmail addresses. "That lowers your credibility in my eyes," he says. "Especially when it is so easy to get an email address with your own custom URL."

7. Printed on poor quality paper. "I have a friend who owns a consulting business and charges in the five figures for their services." Tyrell-Smith says. "When I got their new

business card recently, I was disappointed to pick it up and realize (instantly) what cheap paper they used. Please don't 'cheap out' on the paper. Your brand matters to people. And often the first and early impressions are based on things like your business card. Would I pay $10,000 to someone who has a paper-thin business card? Would you?"

8. Shares too much information. A business card is no place for your elevator pitch; it is just a place to entice people. Draw them in so they can learn more about your business or services. Don't tell your life story.

9. Includes no brand promise or tagline. You need to have a clear and compelling brand promise; without one, your card is simply a contact card—and a not very interesting contact card, at that.

10. Doesn't use the back of the card. "I believe in white space (room around the content that makes your card easier to read) so I always recommend you use the back side of the card," Tyrell-Smith concludes. "If you put your brand promise on the back, you can hand someone your card with that side facing up"—while saying the brand promise out loud.

Signs of the Times

I believe life is a series of near misses. A lot of what we ascribe to luck is not luck at all. It's seizing the day and accepting responsibility for your future. It's seeing what other people don't see and pursuing that vision.   --Howard Schultz

Unless you are of a certain age, gender, or demographic—you probably don't have a clue as to whom Michelle Phan is. No worries. Her 7 million YouTube subscribers know who she is.

So do the 3 million people that like her on Facebook.

So do the honchos at L'Oreal, who gave Phan her own makeup line, Em.

So do her bankers, who say her businesses are worth over $100 million.

Simply put, Phan is the face of a new generation. She's done for the makeup industry what Martha Stewart did for home decorating and Richard Simmons did for exercising.

Phan has made make up—more specifically, the art of applying your own makeup, and doing it well—accessible to the multitudes. Or, as she says, "I'm passionate about being a makeup artist and teaching others how to look and feel fabulous in their own skin."

And she accomplished all of the above long before her 30th birthday. Phan's success is rooted in rejection. Her mother, Jennifer, an immigrant from Vietnam, arrived in America with $20 in her pocket and a burning desire to succeed. She couldn't speak English so the jobs most readily available to her were in nail salons. Michelle grew up watching her mother work, marveling at how she was able to help women feel more beautiful simply by doing their eyebrows or giving them manicures and pedicures. It was a powerful lesson: Changing how a woman looked was the first step towards changing how she felt on the inside.

Phan's family may have been part of the working poor--they lived in one room and received food stamps--but Michelle had big dreams. She loved experimenting with makeup and, at the age of 19, applied for a job at the makeup counter in a large department store. She was turned down.

Instead of sulking, Michelle saw this as a sign that she needed to do something else. She took to the Internet. Since the family didn't own a computer, she started blogging about makeup on a computer at a community college.

In 2007 she took to YouTube, posting videos that showed teens and young women how to apply makeup to achieve whatever look they desired. Phan enrolled in school, getting as far as her junior year at the Ringling College of Art and Design when opportunity came a calling. Impressed by the following that she'd amassed online, in 2010 cosmetic giant Lancôme offered Phan the opportunity to work with them, and she took it. Her YouTube viewership continued to grow, as did her status her reach, and her entrepreneurial spirit. In 2011 Phan became one of the founders of ipsy, an online beauty community. She was also the founder of ICON, a digital lifestyle magazine. More corporate validation followed in 2013 when L'Oreal, the world's largest beauty and cosmetics company, gave her carte blanche to create her own makeup line.

Some viewed Phan's ascension as a cultural shift. "YouTube content creators like Michelle Phan have completely transformed the way people learn about and shop for makeup today," said Google vice president Jim Lecinski, "A few years ago, people primarily shopped by going to the beauty counter at a mall. Now, they go first to YouTube and search for tutorials and reviews."

Ironic, isn't it? Losing out on that cosmetic salesperson job helped launch Phan into a completely different stratosphere. But the ironies don't end there. Assuming that she'd never find the time to complete her coursework, Ringling College honored Phan with an honorary doctorate in 2014.

But in a way, her coursework had already been completed. "The funny thing is that the final project I was working on junior year was a makeup line," Phan said in an interview with The Fashion Spot, an online website. "It's crazy… there is destiny, but I think you also have to make your own destiny. You have to truly believe in it and find all the signs that the universe gives you. So, that's what I did. I kept my eyes open, and looked for all these signs in life."

Today I will be aware of the signs around me.

H.I.T. Parade, Part 1

There's a four-letter word you must use when you get
rejected: NEXT!   --Jack Canfield

Do you have an idea for a new business, invention, or work of art? Is there a story in your soul, a song in your heart, or a new way that you've devised to tackle an old problem? Well, whether you're unemployed, underemployed, or just plain old fashioned uninspired, there's no time like the present to take a stab at it. And after you take that first stab at it, keep on stabbing, even if you hear howls from the naysayers. If nothing else, history teaches us that greatness seldom comes without a struggle. Or rejection. So through it all, if there's a dream in your spirit, your charge is simple: H.I.T.-- Hang In There. And while you're hanging, remember that:

The president of Western Union refused to spend $100,000 to purchase the patent for the telephone from Alexander Graham Bell, declaring that it was nothing but a "toy."

James Whistler failed at West Point and in business before a friend encouraged him to try his hand at painting.

In 1906, Henry Ford's largest investor sold his stock because he didn't think that the company was going anywhere. Ford managed to go broke five times before his motor company became a success.

Gone With the Wind was rejected 38 times before it was finally published.

While in college, Steve Jobs tried to get Atari and Hewlett-Packard interested in his personal computer--even offering to give it to them and work for them if they just paid him a salary--and both companies rejected him. Jobs went on to start Apple.

In 1962, Decca Recording company didn't like this group's sound and thought that guitar music was "on the way out," so the Beatles went elsewhere. They went elsewhere, however, after Columbia records also rejected them.

Alex Haley received 200 rejection notices before his historical novel, *Roots*, became a bestseller.

Today I will H.I.T. no matter what.

Knowing What You Don't Know

If nothing ever changed, there'd be no butterflies.

--Unknown

In the 1980s, Lisa Price worked as a writer's assistant on The Cosby Show. Good job, nice paycheck, lasting benefits (She met her future husband there). Like a lot of us, though, Lisa's passion was totally unrelated to her line of work; she loved fragrances. More specifically, Price loved experimenting with oils and scents—so after work, she made fragrances and body lotions in her kitchen that she gave out as holiday or birthday gifts. She listened, however, when customers told her that what they really wanted were hair care products, made with natural ingredients. Price experimented some more, and by 1993 she was bottling and selling hair care products as well as fragrances at local flea markets.

In 1999, she opened her first retail store in Brooklyn. And today the company begun in Price's kitchen, which she named Carol's Daughter in honor of her mother, is in hundreds of locations nationwide-- including Target and Ulta Beauty. The company's worth is estimated to be in excess of $100 million.

Not bad for an initial $100 investment.

But growth requires change. And change sometimes means handing the reins to others for a while. Price's skill was in creating the product; selling the product was another story. She initially recognized this when her store in Brooklyn was in danger of not meeting payroll. Price discussed the situation with a cousin, who worked for the company, and the cousin came up with this idea: Send out an e-mail blast offering lifetime club memberships to Carol's Daughter—and a 10% discount off of all purchases—to anyone who joined that weekend.

The cost of membership was $25, and the plan worked. That weekend the company generated over $14,000 on the Internet—more than enough to meet payroll.

Yes, there is growth…and then there is growth.

By 2004, Price realized that she'd need to make another change. As she told one magazine, there comes a point "when you feel like, 'OK, this is all that we can do on our own. We've laid the groundwork. We've built this up to this point. And it's in a good place--but it's time to pass the baton so that this can keep going.'" For Price, that meant taking on partner Steve Stoute, whose investment provided more money for website development, packaging, and bringing in a PR firm.

His marketing expertise raised the bar by bringing in celebs like Mary J. Blighe and Jada Pinkett Smith to endorse or invest in the brand. "We just sort of put that viral thing on steroids," Price says. In doing so, the company reached yet another level.

The message is clear: Regardless of how talented, driven, gifted you are—no one can do it all, just as no one can go it alone. Almost as important as knowing what you know is knowing what you don't know… then having the courage to reach out for help. That's a sign of growing up.

And when you grow up, chances are your business will grow as well. That's a change you can believe in all the way to the bank.

Today I will take a look at what I don't know.

Facing the Fallout

Life is 10% of what happens to me and 90% of how I react to it.
                                                    --John Maxwell

Doesn't it seem as if life's tempo alternates between moving at warp speed and hardly moving at all? Occasionally--like when you're waiting for a call to come from a potential employer or when you're bored to tears and waiting for the workday to end--each second seems to last an eternity. But more often than not, the opposite seems to be true: time flies. Blink once--and the work world has changed. Businesses that existed for generations have gone the way of the dinosaur; new businesses appear in their stead from sectors that didn't even exist ten years ago. What the Industrial Age was to the 20th century, the Technological Age is to the 21st century, causing seismic changes in the way business is done. Consultant and change-management adviser James Feldman calls it a shift. And in his aptly titled book *Shift Happens*, Feldman explains it this way: "Shift happens because it is being forced upon us, not because we want it. It is the speed of change, not our acceptance of it that is creating the current shift...

"However, once 'shift' begins, it can gather momentum like a snowball rolling downhill. We are trying to outrun the 'shift' but are getting buried in an avalanche of change."

It's not a good thing to be buried--particularly while you're alive. It is not good to fall victim to circumstances beyond your control. It is not a happy-face, touchy, feel-good place to be.

Now here's the but.

Although the circumstances may be beyond your control, you still have supreme control over the most important thing in the world: You.

A few years back, kids used to proclaim, "You're not the boss of me!" Which simply translates into this: Back off. Back up. I got this. I'm my own boss. I'm the boss of me.

Just as you are the boss of you.

And being your own boss means taking control. It means that despite the avalanche--indeed, from somewhere deep within the avalanche--you still control your thoughts and, as John Maxwell so succinctly put it, your reactions.

The avalanche arrived. It's here. Now what? Well, James Feldman's acronym may come in handy. During the fallout, Feldman says, ask yourself one simple question: Will you Stay Happy In Frightening Times? Can you, will you...shift?

Only you can provide the answer.

Today I will shift my focus to what I can control.

Mother of Invention

It can be liberating to get fired because you realize the world doesn't end. There are other ways to make money, better jobs.

--Ron Livingston

A few years ago, if you looked up the words "having it all," in the dictionary, you might have seen Nichole Hunn's face next to the definition. She was happily married, the mother of three small children. She had a house in the 'burbs. And for more than a dozen years Hunn had been a successful lawyer with an international law firm. Aside from the fact that one of her children had celiac disease (the inability to digest foods with gluten in them--like breads, pasta, cookies), Hunn's life was a piece of cake.

Well, the cake crumbled in March 2009 when Hunn lost her job. Instantly, the pricey gluten-free (GF) diet that her son was on became economically prohibitive. Hunn began blogging about her predicament, and at the same time she started researching and creating inexpensive gluten-free recipes, which she also shared on the web.

Said Hunn: "I figured I couldn't be the only one feeling the strain, could I? Was I the only one longing for good-tasting foods that were safe to eat, simple to make and didn't break the bank? Ones that the whole family--GF and non-GF members alike--could eat and enjoy?"

Clearly, Hunn was not alone. And when *The New York Times* mentioned her blog in an article about the celiac disease, Hunn's life took yet another turn. A literary agent contacted her about turning her blog into the cookbook, within two weeks a publishing company bought exclusive rights to the book, and, voila, a new career was launched. Hunn's first book, *Gluten Free on a Shoestring*, was published almost two years to the day after she lost her job at the international law firm. She has since appeared on radio and TV shows and has been featured in newspaper and magazine articles. Additionally, her brand has grown—with the 2016 release of *Gluten-Free Small Bites*—she currently has five books to her credit.

"Now I spend my time doing what I love," Hunn says. "Developing new recipes, writing about it, and hopefully helping others realize that gluten-free can and should be enjoyable...and affordable."

Today I will note areas in my life
where a change may lead to invention.

#gettingnoticed

Using technology to aid your job search

Making Moves on Social Media

According to a 2015 survey done by the social recruiting site Jobvite, 92 % of recruiters use social media as part of their hiring process; 87 % are using LinkedIn, 55% are using Facebook, 47% are using Twitter. Take home message: It's probably a good idea to get your social media game in order. Facebook (300 million active users), Google Plus (359 million active users) and Twitter (284 million monthly users) are three of the top social media outlets; content marketer Kimberly Barnes offers the following advice when it comes to diving into the social media waters.

Facebook

Find the link: "Research the hiring manager for a company you'd like to work for. Look for friends or friends of friends you share. You can ask for referrals through them, or contact that hiring manager directly," Barnes says.

Spread the word: Now is not the time to be shy; if you're unemployed, everyone needs to know that you're on the job hunt. All your friends will see your status updates, so let them know you're in the market. These updates are easily shared, and you could reach a broader audience.

Join groups related to your field: And if you have an opportunity to help someone with a referral, do it. What goes around comes around may definitely apply—in a good way—if you do so.

Google Plus

Use your words: Key in on keywords – as with LinkedIn, it'll make you more searchable. "Search Google for the jobs you want, and use terms you see there in your profile. Link to your resume and other social media accounts," Barnes advises.

Customize your URL: Barnes advises that you visit gplus.to to change your URL from a set of numbers to your name. She says that it will be easy to remember, will look better as an email tagline, and the link can easily be embedded on your other social media sites.

Tell your story: "Tell your employment history and aspirations with more personality in your 'about' section than you typically would on a resume, cover letter or even on LinkedIn," Barnes says. "Google will display some contacts in your G+ Circles and show those you share in common with a recruiter who finds you via search."

Link it Up: Connect your work and online portfolio in your Google+ profile. But leave out your address or phone number; an email link is safer and should suffice.

Twitter

Follow the company line: Seek out the companies you want to work for. See their job listings and contact them directly. Engage with companies similar to them. Twitter will suggest others in the industry to follow, too.

Loosen up: Says Barnes: "Showcase your personality. Don't be stuffy, be clever. Twitter can be casual. Learn about company objectives from their official accounts, and discern the work culture from those who work there."

Dream big: Find those who do what you want to do – and follow them. Create pertinent content, and turn those contacts into followers. Include portfolio and links to LinkedIn and Google+ profiles.

Cracking the ATS Code, Part 1

Back in the day, here's how you'd go about getting a job. 1) You'd fill out a job application (WAY back in the day, it was on papyrus... uh, I mean paper) 2) You'd hand or mail the application in 3) If you were lucky, you'd get a call from someone who read your application and deemed you worthy enough to follow up with 4) You'd go in for a face-to-face interview or interviews. You were on your way.

Not so today.

Since most jobs today require that you apply online, there's a system in place to accept or reject your resume even before it even has a chance to be seen by human eyes. That system is called the Applicant Tracking System. (ATS).

"Once a resume ends up in electronic form, it becomes a needle in the company's haystack of resumes," notes Abby Kohut, a former human resources executive who now helps job seekers on their quest to find employment through her website www.absoluteabby.com, "While you may think it's a recruiter's job to find you, you MUST realize that it's actually YOUR job to try to be found." Kohut says that some ways to crack the ATS code include:

Becoming Keyword conscious.   Keywords are special words that the hiring company uses in its job listing to highlight what they're looking for in their ideal job candidate. It's important that your submission mirrors those keywords so that the ATS keeps your application in the mix. But even before you get to that point, you need to determine what keywords are truly germane to you. A creative way to figure out your most important keywords, Kohut says, is to pretend you are a recruiter who is searching for you. Without looking at your resume, take five minutes to brainstorm and write down the 20-40 keywords that you think should be included. Review your resume and highlight the keywords you find while you cross each off your list. Then find a way to weave any leftover keywords into your resume. Try the same brainstorming session with a friend who is in the same industry or who has the same kind of job - you'll end up with twice as many keywords in addition to a new job search buddy.

Knowing Your Number. If you are applying for a specific position, make sure that you enter the correct job code because this helps the applicant tracking system put you in the correct bucket. If you use the wrong job code, your resume may get kicked out of the bucket, never be found.

Alleviating abbreviating. Kohut says that if you are "proficient in Word and Excel," your application should say that you are "proficient in Microsoft Word & Microsoft Excel." Ditto saying you know "Office" vs. "Microsoft Office." Why? "A recruiter (using the ATS) cannot search the words "office", "word" or "excel" because they are too common on a resume – people excel at their jobs, work in an office, and type 40 words a minute." Kohut says. "They will have to add the word Microsoft to make the search useful." And if Microsoft isn't on your application, then in that recruiter's search, your application won't show up.

Spell well. Seems pretty basic, doesn't it? If there are free form fields in the application where you have to enter in school names, company names or references, be sure that you spell them correctly. This is not just because spelling errors will make you look sloppy; a misspelled word may also mean a missed keyword matching opportunity.

Cracking the ATS Code, Part 2

When you apply for positions online, keep in mind that the very first "eyes" that see your application probably won't be eyes at all…it will be a computer. And that computer's Applicant Tracking System (ATS) will toss your application quicker than a hot potato if there's something wrong with it, so it behooves you to make sure that your application and your resume are on point. Here are eight tips to keep in mind; and when in doubt, remember to KISS. Keep It Simple, Silly.

1. **Don't choke the ATS.** Pictures, graphics, and logos may look nice on your computer screen, but they are sometimes difficult for the ATS software to sort out… which, in turn, means your application may never make it into human hands. KISS, kiss, kiss!

2. **Do use proper punctuation and capitalization.** Seems like a no-brainer, but it's worth noting that poor punctuation and crazy capitalization can confuse the ATS about where to begin and end a field. If that doesn't lead to outright rejection, it may cause your application to land on the desk of a recruiter or hiring manager who probably won't take kindly to your carelessness.

3. **Don't cut and paste your resume.** When given the option, always upload your resume; often, the computer will highlight and save relevant keywords as the document is uploaded. On the other hand, cutting and pasting your resume—or sending your resume as a PDF—is a tried and true way of choking the system.

4. **Do shout out referrals.** In general, resumes that have landed in the system as a result of employee referrals are looked upon slightly more favorably; after all, an employee isn't likely to put her reputation on the line by recommending a numbskull for a job. If someone at the company you're applying to can vouch for you, make sure the ATS knows it.

5. **Don't wax grandiloquent.** Now is not the time to show off your vocabulary. Label your work experience "Work Experience." Calling it "Professional Achievements," for example, may cause the ATS to skip over your job history because it didn't recognize that it was work related. Yes, that sounds silly…but do you really want to leave it to a computer to decipher what you wrote? I don't think so. KISS!

6. **Do spell things out.** Someone reading your application may be able to figure out that "Mgr" means manager—but don't rely on the computer to make that leap. Just as

with punctuation and capitalization, the ATS needs everything made easy peasy.

7. **Don't omit "optional" information.** In the real world, optional means that you have a choice—not so in the job-seeking world. Experts say that recruiters often use optional information to filter through applications; the more that is known about you, the better.

8. **Do follow-up—even if rejected.** If your best efforts result in one of those awful, automatically-generated rejection e-mails, reach out to the rejecting organization for someone, even a sympathetic administrative assistant, who can tell you the best way to replace the resume currently in the ATS with one containing better keywords and phrases. At the end of the day, although the ATS needs to be respected, nothing trumps the human touch!

Using LinkedIn on the Down Low, Part 1

The good news about LinkedIn is that it is seen and used by hundreds of thousands of employers.

The bad news about LinkedIn is that your boss may be among those hundreds of thousands of employers.

Letting your boss know that you're in the market for a new job is usually not a great career move, so getting LinkedIn on the down low becomes imperative. Susan Joyce, who presides over a 13,000-member group on LinkedIn called Job-Hunt Help as well as a website called Job-Hunt.org, has seen many cases where job hunters "outed" themselves online and got fired by their current employers. It doesn't have to be that way. "When you join any group on LinkedIn, you have the option of including that group's logo in your profile," she says. "With a job-hunting group, don't. And whatever you do, if you already have a job, don't use phrases like 'Seeking a position as…' in your profile or anywhere else." Some other suggestions:

- Stay off the Feed. Change your privacy settings so that your activity is not automatically broadcast to your network in the news feed and so that your network cannot see your activity feed in your profile.

- Avoid contact settings that tip your hand. In the upper right corner of your LinkedIn profile, underneath your picture, is a link to privacy control settings. Here, among other things, you can control who sees your information as well as block people from viewing your profile.

- Ensure that your public profile is fully visible in LinkedIn and search engine results. Here's how: Once you've signed in to your account, click on your name or picture in the upper right hand corner of the screen and click on Privacy and Settings in the dropdown menu. Find "profile" in the bottom section of this settings page and then "helpful links" to the right; click on edit your public profile, then select "Make my public profile visible to everyone". Check the boxes for all the profile content you want to allow others to search for and see. Your settings will be saved automatically.

- Disguise your current employer's name on your resume. Instead of naming the company where you work now, use a generic description. Says Joyce, "Let's say for example that you work for IBM. In place of IBM on your resume, put 'global Fortune 50 information technology company.'" That way, although prospective employers can probably guess what you mean, at least if a manager or recruiter at Big Blue enters "IBM" in a database or job board search field, your name won't pop right up.

- Be conveniently accessible. Once the right people have found you, you want to make it easy for them to reach out to you. Here's how: Once you've signed into your account, click on your name or picture in the upper right hand corner, then click on "Privacy and settings" in the dropdown menu; click on communications to the right, then "Member Communications" to the right. Click on "Select the types of messages you're willing to receive;" select "Introductions and InMails Only." Also, be sure to check the boxes of all the different types of messages you are willing to receive, including "career opportunities."

- Let Google track employers and opportunities for you. Expand the scope of your online search beyond LinkedIn by compiling a list of companies where you might like to work and signing up for free Google alert. This way, you'll be notified when jobs are posted on those organizations' web sites or when Google picks up news about an employer that may be useful to you. And, just to state the obvious--have those alerts sent to your home email address, not to your office.

Using Linked In On the Down Low, Part 2

You need only look at the Equifax data breach of 2017 to know that nothing these days is truly private…including those "privacy" settings in LinkedIn. "The confusion arises when LinkedIn users see the option for a Public Profile and believe its purpose is to lock down information," says executive resume writer Laura Smith-Proulx. What that setting does, however, is simply prevent access to your profile's URL by someone using an outside search engine like Google, Bing or Yahoo. But anyone who is already LinkedIn only needs to have a 1st or 2nd degree connection to you in order to access all the information in your profile. Smith-Proulx tells of other ways that LinkedIn is not so on the down low.

You are eminently searchable. Anyone who is already LinkedIn can use the site's search function at the top of the page to find you…and they don't even need to remember your full name. "LinkedIn allows searches on People, Companies, Universities, or Groups, so that users can quickly drill through the results," says Smith-Proulx. "When other users find you, 100% of the information you put on your Profile is visible to them, as long as they're connected to you (1st and 2nd-degree connections). Those outside of your network will just see your name." Sounds OK, right? Alas…

You can't control the actions of your network. "All it takes for you to become a 2nd-degree connection away from someone else (your boss, for example) is for someone in your circle to connect with that person," says Smith-Proulx. So while refusing to connect with colleagues or supervisors on LinkedIn may work for a while, if either your network or their network expands, end of story. Instantly, they can become closer to you on LinkedIn with full access to see your profile.

Activity "broadcast" settings only prevent notifications to other users. If you don't want to announce changes to your profile to the co-workers you're connected to on LinkedIn, you can go the privacy controls and uncheck the box labeled "Let people Know when you change your profile, make recommendations, or follow other users." But this only removes the announcement of the change, not the change itself. If your boss or co-workers are monitoring your profile, they will be able to see your revisions. "Keep this in mind when adding new data on LinkedIn, since there's no way to "lock down" your profile and prevent spying eyes from viewing your information," says Smith-Proulx. But that shouldn't come as much of a surprise to you; after all, the purpose of LinkedIn is to let others know about you and your skills. So remember that preventing access to your profile can be difficult to do, and proceed accordingly.

Apps that Help Your Job Search

Although features vary, job search apps usually send alerts about new postings, giving you a heads up on other job seekers. Some apps use your phone's GPS to notify you of job openings in your area. Other apps allow you to apply for or at least signal interest in a job… all through your mobile device.

Here are seven free apps you may want to consider downloading.

Glassdoor Job Search—If you're targeting a job within a specific company or looking for a specific salary range, this app is a good one. You can receive push notifications as soon as new jobs are found in your category. When you tap on a specific job opening, this app will take you to the page of detailed information. One of this app's differentiating features is that you can get the inside scoop on companies, via the opinions of current and former employees.

LinkedIn Job Search—This app recommends jobs based on the keywords you entered in your profile. You can get automatic recommendations and notifications based on previous job searches. It also allows for location-based searches. And there's the guarantee of total privacy—your network won't hear a thing about your in-app activity.

Indeed Job Search—This app's database has over 16 million jobs, and you can view new jobs added since your last search. You can search by job title, company, and location to find your dream job. Fulltime, part time, contract, freelance and internship jobs are available. You can create a resume and personal message for each job before applying.

ZipRecruiter--Enter your desired location, keywords or job titles and this app will scour over 100 job boards at once. Apply for jobs with just one tap; you'll be notified when your resume has been viewed. If you're not ready to pull the trigger just yet, this app will save your job searches so you can come back to them at a later time. Additionally, best-matched jobs are delivered to your mailbox daily.

Job Search—SnagAJob—Specializing in hourly employment jobs, this app features more than a million full time and part time jobs in industries like restaurant, retail, hospitality and customer service. Use your SnagAJob profile to apply for jobs in just one click or use video to personalize your profile. This app lets you view real-time updates on the status of your application.

Monster.com Job Search—Search, view and apply to jobs immediately or save/email them to apply later. You can upload your resume via Dropbox or Google Drive. Receive push notifications and/or e-mail alerts for new jobs that fit your criteria.

Quadjobs—This one is for college students. Quadjobs (available right now in select cities) answers the perennial question of how to get a job without experience even though you can't get experience without a job. Ranging from dog walking to retail or tech positions, these jobs may offer the connections and the opportunity for a student to step into the workforce so that he or she can eventually step up.

Apps that Work Anonymously

Although you may be feeling as snug as a bug in a rug in your job right now, these two apps may anonymously help you uncover new opportunities. After all, everyone knows that the best time to look for a new job is when you already have one… even if, technically, you're not looking for a new job at all.

Anthology— Write down what it would take for you to move from your current job to another one—salary, title, location, seniority, benefits, size of company—and the app will screen opportunities for you. Using "advanced machine learning algorithms" to predict potential matches among its 1,000 plus recruiters, you'll get notified only if there is a solid match. At that point, the ball is in your court; you can confirm your interest anonymously, and if the employer is also interested, you can reveal your identity to the employer and take it from there.

Switch— Upload your profile and in minutes you may review jobs Switch recommends based on your background and location. Swipe right to "like" a job, and swipe left to pass. When a hiring manager of a job you liked is interested in you, Switch connects you directly via email or chat. Switch will not show jobs listed by your current employer—nor will your current employer be able to see your profile.

Dare to Do You

The best way to change your belief system is to change the truth about you. What you actually do is more important than what you say you'll do.
                                        --Steve Chandler

Have you ever heard the expression "Talking loud and saying nothing?"

That's what a lot of us are guilty of, especially when it comes to how we handle our feelings of dissatisfaction about our jobs. On the one hand, sometimes we're happy to at least have a piece of a job, with the unemployment rates being what they are and all. But on the other hand, there's a whole lot of yada going on.

This job is beneath me; I gotta get out of here. Yada, yada yada.

My employers don't respect me; I gotta get outta here. Yada, yada, yada.

I work with a bunch of numbnuts; I gotta get outta here. Yada, yada, yada.

There's a reason why we say that talk is cheap. It costs nothing to run your mouth--nothing but the energy you expend doing it and the time your family and friends expend listening to you mouth off. But what does that babble accomplish, other than give voice to your frustrations and demonstrate your total lack of gratitude? A wise person once said that a little bit of something is better than a whole lot of nothing. And grumbling about your predicament certainly doesn't get you any closer to where you want to be.

So maybe your job isn't brain surgery--but hopefully it is helping fill up your car's gas tank. And maybe you're not working in the field that you went to school for or, even worse, maybe you're working at something that you never wanted to do--but you're working nonetheless. So you can either suck it up and deal with it, or find a way to get another job. But please, stop kvetching about how much you hate your job. Back in the day, Nike's advertising campaign admonished us to "Just do it."

Same could be said here. When it comes to changing your work environment, don't talk about it...be about it!

There's no time like the present to dare to do you!

Today I will tone down the rhetoric and actually do something.

Taking Bliss to the Bank

There is a vast world of work out there where at least 111 million people are employed in this country alone, many of whom are bored out of their minds. All day long. --Richard Nelson Bolles

Perhaps you have a hobby that you're passionate about. Collecting Batman comics, snowboarding, baking cupcakes—the hobby isn't important, your love of it is. Because if you're working the 9-5 at a job you don't particularly care for, that hobby may be just what you need to keep you from going completely bonkers. Plus there's this: whatever the economy, pursuing your bliss—even on a part time basis—can put pennies in your pocket. Maybe even more. Case in point: Gary Vaynerchuk.

Vayenrchuk's parents owned a brick and mortar discount liquor store in Springfield Township, N.J., and Gary worked there on weekends while in college. Although his first love had always been sports, Gary quickly recognized that collecting wines was a little bit like collecting baseball cards, so he switched teams, as it were. His learning curve of the wine industry coincided with the rise of social media, and Vaynerchuk wisely combined the two.

In 1997 Gary launched Winelibrary.com, which helped the family business grow from $3 million to $45 million in sales by 2005. That same year, he began video blogging and in 2006 he started Winelibrary.TV, where his reviews of wines attracted 100,000 viewers a day.

In 2009 he wrote *Crush It: Why Now Is the Time To Cash in on your Passion*, and also teamed with brother A.J. to form VaynerMedia, an agency that helps Fortune 500 companies (like PepsiCo and the Campbell Soup Company) find their social media voices and build their digital brands. By the time his second book, *The Thank You Economy*, was published in 2011, Vaynerchuk had close to a million followers on Twitter. Today, Vaynerchuk is a sought after public speaker, a venture capitalist, and a four-time *New York Times* bestselling author who has been named to both *Crain's* and *Fortune's* 40 Under 40 lists.

And it all began with wine.

The kicker, according to Vaynerchuk, is that you can do something similar, although perhaps in a slightly smaller vein, in your niche.

"Not everyone is going to be Oprah," Vaynerchuk says, "But the fact that someone can make enough money for a family vacation—and talk about the Cincinnati Reds because that's the thing they love the most—they need to wrap their head around that."

*Today I will explore if what makes me happy
can also make me money.*

Change Up!

So what do we do? Anything. Something. So long as we just don't sit there. If we wait until we've satisfied all the uncertainties, it may be too late. If we screw it up, start over. Try something else.

--Lee Iacocca

You've probably heard this one before: The definition of insanity is doing the same thing over and over again and expecting different results. That definition doesn't just hold true for your actions; it also applies to your attitude.

Think about it. If your attitude when you get up every morning is "Ho-hum, here goes another boring day," chances are you'll return to bed that evening having lived through another boring, ho-hum day. If your attitude at work is "I could care less about this job, I'm just here for the paycheck," chances are you're going to get absolutely nothing out of your job but a paycheck.

If your attitude towards life in general is "Hey, I'm just making it from day to day," chances are that one day will turn into another day, and then another month, and then another year and then all of the sudden you'll be toothless, 96 years old, and wondering where the time went and what the hell happened. Where's the joy in that?

Here's a clue: It isn't there.

What if, instead, you actually did something to shake your world up? What if you got out of bed in the morning saying that this was going to be a stupendous, momentous, fantabulous day…and then went out and tried to make it so? Your day might not reach the stupendous level--but it's a good bet that it would beat the pants off of ho-hum.

What if you went to work looking to do more than pick up a paycheck? Who knows… you might actually pick up a new skill or make a new contact or discover a new tidbit about your place of employment that you didn't know about before.

And what if you decided that you weren't satisfied with merely making it from day to day? What if you resolved to escape the monotony of your daily routine and try to shake things up--to explore someplace new, create something different, spend time with someone special, play a sport, laugh, love, giggle, have fun?

What if you decided to…drum roll, please. Actually live?

Wow…what a concept!

Today I will go for the gusto

The Little Engine that Could

The best way to not feel hopeless is to get up and do something. Don't wait for good things to happen to you. If you go out and make some good things happen, you will fill the world with hope, you will fill yourself with hope.   --Barack Obama

She was an overweight people pleaser who wanted everyone to like her. An under-the-radar C student who became a struggling single mother on public assistance…in South Central L.A., no less. She was almost a living, breathing, cliché. But a scenario that could have turned into disaster instead transformed into success. Today's eight-letter word is this: Tenacity. "I am an example of the Little Engine that Could--the engine that didn't have the best mechanics or tires, but the engine wouldn't stop. That's the engine that I think that I'm an example of."

Meet Lisa Nichols, CEO of Motivating the Masses, Inc., one of the top training and development companies in the world. She's a best-selling author and transformational speaker whose global platform has reached and served millions. But who the heck wakes up one day deciding that they want to be a motivational speaker? Certainly not Nichols.

What she realized, however, was that she had the gift of gab and the heart and spirit that wanted to make a difference in the world, particularly in the lives of teenagers.

"I had no idea what the financial value would be, but I knew what the human value would be…. My whole intent was I wanted to save teen lives, one teen at a time," Nichols says of her soul's desire. "I said I was going to give 18 free workshops. Well, on my 42nd free workshop, I thought, 'Hmmm… Maybe this plan needs to be revised.'"

What's interesting about this situation is that Nichols gave those free workshops at a time that she desperately needed income. "My son and I were eating cabbage, carrots, and onions— that's what we had in our refrigerator at one point—so all I could make was stir fry," Nichols says. "I didn't have money to give away, but I did have a skill. I had been gifted with the skill of facilitation and teaching people how to turn breakdowns into breakthroughs." She used that skill the best she could and eventually actually began getting paid for her talents. Her influence grew. According to her website, Nichols' "Motivating the Teen Spirit" workshops have impacted over 200,000 teens, prevented 800 suicides and encouraged over 575 drop outs to return to school. Featured in the self-development movie, The Secret (2006), Nichols' book, *No Matter What*, was a NYT bestseller. And her transformational work with adults has reached millions.

So what does this mean for you? Just like The Little Engine that Could, Nichols' take-home message is old school to the core: What goes around comes around.

"Life is a cycle; everything is on a big wheel. You give good, you need to know it's coming back. You give something else, you need to know it's coming back," Nichols says. "Create a value in who you are—your intellectual property, your time, your contribution, what you do—and it will begin to come back to you."

Today I will recognize that there is no lack in my life;
I can make my mark wherever I am.

Age Ain't Nothin' But a Number, Pt. 2

The only place where your dream becomes impossible is in your own thinking.   --Robert Schuller

He grew up in Hong Kong and was 11-years-old when he began by selling candy to neighborhood kids for a profit.

She grew up in Austin, Texas and was 4 ½ years old when she opened a lemonade stand on her front lawn, using her great grandmother's secret recipe to attract customers.

When he earned his first $1.97 online—he became hooked on using the Internet as a way to make money.

When she realized that she could help save bees from extinction, and run a profitable business at the same time –she became hooked on using lemonade as a way to make money.

In many respects, Stanley Tang and Mikaila Ulmer are worlds apart, but in one respect they are similar: At very young ages, they knew what they wanted out of life—and went for it. In the innocence of their youth, they were wise enough to realize that age ain't nothing but a number.

Tang attributes his entrepreneurial awakening to *Rich Dad, Poor Dad* by Robert Kiyosaki, which he read in 2005. "It was the first time I ever realized the vast amount of opportunities there was in the world of business and entrepreneurship – and that there were other options besides getting a safe, secure job and climbing the corporate ladder for the rest of my life," Tang says.

In 2006, Tang registered his first domain name and began creating niche, content-rich websites that focused on web hosting, magic tricks and business. He spent 48 hours writing an eBook called Co-Registration Secrets Revealed, which earned over $2,000 in less than a week. Tang's following and customer base grew to such an extent that between January and December of 2007, his business generated over five figures in sales. Not bad for a 14-year-old.

Since then, Tang has released eMillions (an e-book that debuted at #1 on Amazon.com), reached 100,000 followers on Twitter, launched (and closed) a social news aggregation website called BuzzBlaze, interned at Facebook, and, oh yeah, studied computer science at Stanford University. In 2012 he teamed up with fellow students Andy Fang and Tony Xu and founded Door Dash, a food-delivery service that Tang says is the next generation of on-demand, local delivery. "Ultimately, our vision is to build the local, on-demand Fedex. We are a logisitics company more so than a food company."

Through the DoorDash app, hungry consumers may order from local restaurants and affiliated food chains (like Taco Bell) in more than 70 cities. The company currently employs more than 200 employees. Tang describes himself this way: "I create cool stuff that's innovative, disruptive and elegant and have a passion for engaging in the creative process of building tech startups." You could say that again.

When bees stung Ulmer twice in the same week she became deathly afraid of them. Her parents suggested that she face her fear by learning more about bees; Ulmer discovered that honey bees were great pollinators, but perhaps because of pesticides, they were dying. Right then and there Ulmer decided to do something. She added honey to her great-grandmother's flaxseed lemonade recipe, set up a lemonade stand, and donated a percentage of her profits to organizations that helped save bees.

Then she kicked it into overdrive. Soon neighborhood stores and businesses were selling BeeSweet, the lemonade that Ulmer, her parents, and her brother were bottling in their home. In 2015, after Ulmer and her Dad scored a $60,000 deal with Daymond John on Shark Tank, sales of BeeSweet (renamed Me &The Bees Lemonade) increased 200 and, later, 400 percent. "My lemonade does good," she says, "And it tastes really good."

Through research, education, and preservation, her non-profit Healthy Hive Foundation seeks to increase honeybee awareness as well as the number of safe environments for bees to live in. In 2016—the same year Ulmer introduced President Barack Obama at the United States of Women Summit—her business was worth upwards of $11 million. Me&The Bees is currently sold in over 60 Whole Foods stores nationwide. Today, in addition to being CEO and Founder of Me&The Bees, Ulmer regularly speaks to audiences about the digestive benefits of flaxseed oil, leads workshops on how to save honeybees, and participates in social entrepreneurship panels.

Her advice?

"Don't let your age get to you. Even as kids, we're capable of doing so much. A lot of people think that kids aren't capable of starting their own business, but that's not true--create a business that you're passionate about," Ulmer says. "I always remind myself why I started this company. Of course I want to make money, but I started it to save the bees. And with every bottle that you buy, remember that we're saving the bees.

"Entrepreneur's hold the American dream, and the biggest dreamers are kids," Ulmer concludes. "My advice to anyone who is looking to start a business is simple: Bee fearless. Bee-lieve in the impossible, and dream like a kid."

Today I won't let my age detract me from my goal.

YEAH, I GOT IT
GOIN' ON

Employment tips for younger workers

Advice for Recent College Grads

You went to college, attended classes, amassed tens of thousands of dollars worth of debt, graduated, and now you're broke, busted and living back in the basement of your parent's house. A guy named "Fats" Domino once put it this way: "A lot of fellows nowadays have a B.A., M.D., or Ph.D. Unfortunately, they don't have a J.O.B."

Welcome to your brave new adult world.

In all seriousness, though, eventually you will get a job or start an awesome business. The question is when will it happen and how will you go about making it happen. Three tried and true employment tips for recent college grads include:

Know how to talk about yourself. You may not have much on-the-job experience, but for twenty-something years you have lived a life and so you have life experience. Learn how to toot your own horn; if someone asks who are you and what are you looking for, workwise, what will you say? Practice a response; knowing what you want out of a career indicates that you are a go-getter, and employers like that.

Network. Now that you're an alumnus, put your school's alumni association to good use. Ditto professional organizations; join at least one that is related to your field of interest. Clearly it's not enough to just join—you've also got to attend meetings, meet new people and establish relationships with them. People help people they know. And no one will know you if you spend 99% of your time in the bedroom. Get out there and act like you want to do something with your life!

Be flexible. Truth is that your first job may not be in your field. But does that make it a bad job? Not necessarily. You never know how something is going to work out until you try it. Don't squash an opportunity because it doesn't meld with what your vision for your life is. If you truly can't stand your job, there's always a way out. It's called quitting. Death and taxes are assured; everything else is up for grabs.

When Jeff Bezos, the billionaire founder of Amazon, addressed the Princeton graduating class of 2010, he left them with these words. "I will hazard a prediction," Bezos said. "When you are 80 years old, and in a quiet moment of reflection narrating for only yourself the most personal version of your life story, the telling that will be most compact and meaningful will be the series of choices you have made. In the end, we are our choices. Build yourself a great story."

Reworking Your Resume

Perhaps you're a freshly minted college grad. Or maybe you haven't graduated from college at all, but you want to take a step up the job market ladder. Your dilemma is a common one: Although you've held a job (or jobs) in the past, the skillset gained from your previous employer doesn't match up with the skillset requested for the job you want. Your resume seems woefully off the mark, which means that the odds of actually getting that job lie somewhere between slim and none, right?

Wrong.

Magicians deal in sleight of hand; job seekers deal in sleight of words. Which is not, I repeat, NOT, the same as lying. It's more like spin control on steroids or exhibiting an expansive way with words. And when done the right way, it's a beautiful thing. No one's better at resume prestidigitation Donald Asher, author of *From College to Career*, a remarkable resume book for college students. Here are two examples of Asher's magic; from the descriptions below, see if you can guess what job each applicant currently holds.

Person A's resume (applying for a job in finance):

- Proven ability to deal with a wide range of individuals, including high-net-worth investors and institutional money manager, in a stressful and time-sensitive environment.

- Knowledge of financial markets and instruments, especially stocks, bonds, futures and options.

Person B's resume (applying for an entry-level marketing job):

- Act as a "sales representative" for the restaurant, selling add-ons and extras to achieve one of the highest per-ticket and per-night sales averages.
- Prioritize and juggle dozens of simultaneous responsibilities.
- Have built loyal clientele of regulars in addition to tourist trade.
- Use computer daily.

OK—the big reveal.

Person A is currently working as a receptionist; Person B is currently a waitress. Notice how the description of their current jobs featured buzzwords germane to the jobs they were seeking. After all, the main purpose of a resume is to get you in the door-- but an interviewer won't open the door unless you have something to offer. So be creative and tailor your skills to the job that you are seeking.

Eight Ways to Find a Job

If you want to move on up out of your current situation, the strategy is pretty much the same no matter what your "u" may be: unemployed, underemployed or uninspired. Bottom line is this: you've got to get to steppin'. Beyond the want ads, here are eight ways to job hunt, courtesy of Bankrate.com

1. Use Internet job boards; your best results will likely come from industry-specific job boards.

2. Network through personal contacts; whether you're hitting folks up on your cell or connecting through social networking websites, sometimes it truly isn't about what you know but who you know.

3. Use career consultants; particularly if you're going after higher paying jobs

4. Use recruiters, private agencies; they're helpful not only for heavy hitters, but also for finding temporary or jobs in your particular field of interest.

5. Seek internships; if your pride and your wallet can stand it, getting a foot in the door beats standing outside in the rain.

6. Check out job fairs; again, the more specific they are to your industry, the better.

7. Visit school placement services; if you're still in school, this is a no-brainer. But oftentimes, alums don't realize that many larger schools have career placement services for alums.

8. Look at government positions; USAjobs, fedjobs.gov, and state and local job boards are often great resources. You may be pleasantly surprised at the variety of jobs available on those sites.

Building A Successful Relationship With a Mentor

"The most successful people in the world make a habit of seeking regular guidance and support from experts in their fields," says Jack Canfield. "They do so by seeking mentors."

Most of us know Jack Canfield courtesy of his amazingly successful *Chicken Soup for the Soul* franchise, but nowadays he has gone beyond books and has become a well-respected life coach. Canfield comes by this transition honestly; as a young man, he was mentored by one of America's earliest "see it and be it" proponents, self-made millionaire W. Clement Stone. "He was the first person to declare that I could have and be anything I wanted, despite the challenges I faced being raised by an alcoholic mother and workaholic father in a lower-income blue-collar home," Canfield says. "Stone took me under his wing, introducing me to the success principles I now live and teach."

One of those principles involves getting into a mentor-mentee relationship. But—as the word 'relationship' implies—this interaction is a two way street. While there are many ways that mentors may nurture your professional growth (like providing advice, opening doors, or introducing you to the "right" people), you must also bring something to the table: at minimum, you must display a willingness to grow. Canfield offers the following advice on how to create a successful relationship with a mentor.

Do your research. Not just anyone in your industry will be the right fit for you; do a little homework before asking someone to mentor you. Search the Internet, read industry publications, approach others in your profession for suggestions about who to approach. Look for people with well-rounded experience that would be helpful in tackling your goal.

Be clear about what you want. "Make a list of specific points you'd like to cover during your first conversation, such as why you'd like them to mentor you and what kind of help you'd be looking for," Canfield says. "Be brief, but be confident, too." And be reasonable about your expectations. A mentor probably won't have hours each week to help you, but a short phone call each month might be agreeable.

Ask, ask, ask. Make a list of a few people you'd like to have as a mentor, because your first, second, maybe even your third choice might not have the time to do it. Keep at it though. Sooner or later, someone will give you a positive response.

Act on advice. "Mentors don't like to have their time wasted," Canfield says. "When you seek their advice, follow it. Study their methods, ask your questions, make sure you understand the process, and then do your best to duplicate it."

Return the favor. Turn about is fair play; look for ways to give back to your mentor, such as keeping her updated on technological trends or industry information or by pulling her coattail regarding new opportunities that she might benefit from. And be willing to share with others, too. "It's a human trait to want to pass on wisdom; be willing to help others by sharing what you've learned," Canfield says. "Seeing a former protégé out in the world helping others to grow is one of the best rewards you can give to your mentors."

Seven Rules for Climbing in Your Career

Congratulations! You're young, energetic, and—praise the Lord—employed! And double kudos if you've been fortunate enough land a gig in your chosen field; in that respect, you've truly hit the jackpot! But if you're like most people in your age bracket, in all likelihood that isn't enough. A recent survey by PriceWaterhouse Coopers found that more than half of twenty-something year-old workers want real opportunities for career advancement—and they want it NOW.

"In this 24/7 Internet-connected world, it makes sense that this generation would expect speedier recognition," notes Manhattan-based job interview and image consultant Vicky Oliver. But speedier recognition only happens if it is deserved. And much of what it takes in order to become deserving of greater recognition is never taught in school. Oliver, author of five career-related books (including *301 Smart Answers to Tough Interview Questions*) offers these seven life lessons to live by as you seek to climb your career ladder.

1. Don't feel entitled. "There are now three generations of workers at the workplace. And sporting the entitlement chip can be very off-putting to older workers," Oliver says. No one is entitled to any special perks or plum assignments until after he's proven himself. So come in early, leave late, and respect those

deadlines. Note: Unlike in college, deadlines at work often cannot be pushed back!

2. Pay those dues. In order to scramble to the top rung of the corporate ladder, you have to excel at the bottom. "So don't shirk the boring assignments, and do volunteer for additional work if possible," Oliver says. "Show supervisors and coworkers alike that you're diligent, self-motivated, and reliable."

3. Find a mentor. Seek mentors from the outside if you can't find them on the inside of your company. Look for mentors among your peers at other companies--particularly those who are 5-10 years ahead of you in terms of experience--and who hold the kind of position you would like to occupy in a few years.

4. Work hard. Make your first job your number one priority--above your love life, exercise routine, and hanging out with your friends. And if you don't need it for work, turn off the cell phone when you're in the office. Trust us: It will turn back on when you leave for the day!

5. Lead your own way. Don't look for your boss to carve out your career path. You may get lucky and have a boss who will take a special interest in helping you get ahead. Then again, you may not. You may have to make horizontal career moves a few times before you move up or find the right career trajectory. "With today's "flat" hierarchical structures becoming the norm--i.e. having few if any managers between employees and the top

leaders--you may be expected to define your own leadership role," says Oliver.

6. Hone your people skills. Realize that every business is a people business. Yes, it's essential to be good at the details of your job. But it's even more important to polish those soft skills, including helping others, listening, asking smart questions, not interrupting, being attentive, and getting along.

7. Master the rules, then challenge. Learn the way things are done--and excel at that system and process--before trying to change anything. "Too often, especially when we're first starting out, we believe we know a better way," Oliver says. "Trust that the system in place is probably there for a reason. If it isn't efficient or up-to-date, learn everything about it so you can build a cogent and convincing argument for doing it differently."

Developing Good Career Habits

Bad habits are like bad haircuts—they're everywhere. But if you are serious about taking your work life to the next level, you've got to get rid of them. Caroline Ceniza-Levine, co-founder of the career coaching company SixFigureStart, advises you to do the following:

Start scheduling lunch dates. Find people that you want to connect with—for social reasons or professional networking—and e-mail them now. "But instead of saying 'Let's get together [sometime]' offer a specific date." Aim for 10 dates per quarter. "You can get away one day a week!" Ceniza-Levine says.

Start scheduling resume updates. Again it's a good idea to look at your resume quarterly. Make sure your contact info is updated and all jobs are represented. Says Ceniza-Levine: "Then add your latest projects—since you're doing this every few months, your memory should be pretty accurate. Remember to refine the job descriptions so that they are relevant to what you're interested in today."

Start scheduling training days. Register for your company's offerings; if your company has none, block out a half or full day each month to catch up on professional reading.

Read to trade publications. If your company doesn't have any publications applicable to your industry in the office, take out your own subscriptions; they're usually tax-deductible as a professional expense.

Join trade organizations. "At minimum, you will get newsletters and announcements," Ceniza-Levine says. "It would also be ideal to attend meetings and join a committee."

Gut Check

Get mad, then get over it.   --Colin Powell

Let's assume, for the moment, that you are totally blameless. Your job loss was 1,000 percent not your fault. A rough economy, a company takeover, you name it—whatever the cause, you're an innocent victim. And you're steamed. You gave those so-and-sos some of the best years of your life, and now you've been tossed aside like yesterday's news.

It hurts. You're mad as hell. How could they? How dare they? Don't they know that you have mouths to feed, bills to pay, a life to live? And why the hell did they get rid of you? Everyone knows that [you-fill-in-the-name] does nothing but take up space…yet he/she is still getting paid?? Hell to the no! If you can't legally kick butt and take names, the least you could do is go back to that job and give somebody—preferably your milquetoast boss—a piece of your mind. Right? Uh, wrong…for a variety of reasons.

Newsflash #1: Nobody really cares about your hurt feelings. Your company--make that your former company—is in business to make money and provide a service, probably in that order. For whatever reason, you no longer fit into the equation. It probably isn't personal, but even if it is, this much is certain—your hurt feelings don't matter even a little bit, at least not to the powers that be. Move on.

Newsflash#2: Your name and your reputation will live on long after you've exited the building. So while releasing a plume of profanities may provide you with a momentary feel good moment, it will only come back to haunt you when you need a reference or a recommendation somewhere down the road. Ditto that F-U letter. If you must get your anger down on paper, do so. Then immediately burn the evidence.

Newsflash #3: You are not your job. You may have liked your job, depended on it, grown accustomed to it, identified with it… but get a grip. You are a person. A person who may be slightly frazzled around the edges right now, but you can and you will rise above the situation. Does that mean that you must zip your lip that you can't say what is on your mind? Of course not. People can and should express themselves, as long as they do it appropriately. The rule is this: If you can't say what's on your mind in a civil and sane manner, say nothing.

Remember, you are not your job. You are a person with grace, class, and most of all, control. And the time to exercise that control is now.

Today I will use my anger to fuel my internal fires,
not to lash out at former co-workers.

H.I.T. Parade, Pt. 2

We must be willing to let go of the life we've planned, so as to have the life that is waiting for us.   --Joseph Campbell

Not everyone knows what he or she should be doing from birth. Life happens, and we sometimes wind up in jobs or careers simply because they pay the bills. Pragmatism has its place. But although life may not give you a second chance to make a first impression, it damn sure will give you a second—maybe even a third—chance to live your dream. If one career doesn't float your boat, perhaps you should jump ship and try something else. And after you jump, H.I.T.—Hang In There. Others before you have switched careers and done all right for themselves. For instance:

Harrison Ford had worked as a carpenter for 15 years when George Lucas gave him a small part in his movie *American Graffiti*. Years later, Lucas hired Ford build something in his office; as fate would have it, when an actor was late for a reading, Lucas asked Ford to read the lines for him. Stephen Spielberg was in the room that day and the rest, as they say, is history. Ford landed the starring role in Lucas' film, a little ditty he called *Star Wars*.

Speaking of *Star Wars*, when James Cameron saw that film in 1977, he was a truck driver—but that movie propelled him to quit his day job and begin studying filmmaking. You could say Cameron's been successful: he's won three Oscars and has an estimated worth of $700 million due to films like *Titanic*, *Avatar*, and *The Terminator*.

Andrea Bochelli worked as a lawyer and sang, on the side, at a piano bar. It wasn't until he was in his mid-thirties that this amazing tenor really began pursuing a singing career. Why? "I came to believe that if you have a gift, you have an obligation to share it with others. It's as simple as that." His album, Sacred Arias, is the biggest selling classical album by a solo artist of all time.

Martha Stewart worked as a stockbroker on Wall Street for about five years, until she and her husband bought and moved into an old house in Connecticut. She began renovating that house and, well, you know the rest of the story. Stewart's empire today encompasses television, magazines and home décor, among other things, and her personal worth is estimated to be $650 million.

Finally, this fellow's early resume reads as follows: Went to war as a captain, returned as a private. Failed as a businessman. Was deemed too impractical and temperamental to be a successful lawyer. Ran for political office and was defeated on five separate occasions. After his fifth defeat, he wrote to a friend saying, "I am now the most miserable an living. If what I feel were equally distributed to the whole human family, there would not be one cheerful face on the earth." Who was he? Abraham Lincoln.

Today I will assess whether my career is one of conviction or one of convenience.

Age Ain't Nothin' But a Number, Pt. 3

No one can avoid aging, but aging productively is something else. --Katharine Graham

In a society that reveres all things youthful, anyone over the age of 30 is considered suspect, anyone over the age of 40 is considered senile, and anyone over the age of 50 is considered a candidate to grab a shovel and start digging his or her own grave. Certainly, these are not the best of times for those in their 40s and 50s, particularly when it comes to scouring for jobs in this job market. We may be living longer than ever, but the economy is such that many of us are living on a dollar and a dream. And that dream sometimes turns into a nightmare, particularly when the people doing the hiring are young enough to be our children--or grandchildren.

All of which can lead middle aged job seekers to feel downright dinosauric, poised to be pushed off of the employment merry-go-round long before we want to leave. But even if the ride is dizzying, even if the job search odds seem a little stacked against you, take heart.

Your years have given you experience, your experience has given you knowledge, and your knowledge--the knowledge borne of trial and error and just living life--is something no twenty-something can touch.

So don't lose hope; there is absolutely no validity to the notion that your latter days cannot be greater than your former. In fact, your latter days may take twists and turns that seem antithetical to anything that happened in your youth. Exhibit A in the age ain't nothing but a number scenario is Admiral Joe Fowler.

Admiral Fowler, a veteran of both world wars, retired from the Navy in 1948 at the age of 54. During WWII, Fowler had designed and built the two largest aircraft carriers in the world. A few years into retirement, the age of 60, he met Walt Disney, who convinced Fowler to come and work with him. For the next 25 years Fowler did--first by overseeing the construction (and later managing the operations) of Disneyland in Anaheim California, then by planning and building Walt Disney World in Orlando, Fla. At one point during the Florida project, Fowler held three posts simultaneously, including senior vice president, engineering and construction for Walt Disney productions and director of construction for Disney's Buena Vista Construction Company.

When Fowler really retired--after Epcot Center had been built--he was 84 years old--thirty years beyond his first retirement age. And even at that, he stayed on with Walt Disney World as a consultant.

According to people who knew him, the secret to Fowler's success lay in his two favorite words: "Can do." Would Disneyland be able to open its doors on the date that Walt Disney promised it would open? "Can do." Would the construction and installation of four Disney-themed productions at the 1964 World's Fair be ready in time? "Can do." Whatever situation Fowler was presented with, he responded positively, with a can-do attitude. And remember: this attitude emanated from someone in his sixth, seventh, eighth decade of life. It came from someone keenly aware that age ain't nothin' but a number.

What's your number? Don't worry about it...it's not important. Concentrate on what you know, what you have to offer, what you can do. Develop Fowler's can do spirit. Then take what you can do to the next level... and just do it.

Today I will look to the future with confidence.

Carpe Diem

Seize the moment. Remember all those women on the Titanic who waved off the dessert cart.   --Erma Bombeck

You've got this situation going on in your life. And the situation, to put it bluntly, sucks. I mean it really, truly sucks.

So the question of the moment is simple yet eternal: Now what?

Do you drag your family, neighbors, acquaintances and the dog into that good old fashioned pity party you're throwing for yourself where your featured guests are the ever popular Bitch and Moan? Or do you take the opposite tact and fall into the role of recluse as you silently slink off into sorry seclusion?

Do you try to avoid the situation through—take your pick—drugs, alcohol, food, video games, sex, books, shopping, cooking, cleaning or whatever else your personal escape mechanism happens to be? Or do you tackle the situation so relentlessly that you give yourself migraines?

Or do you take a more measured approach--yet despite your best efforts, the bad situation only seems to get worse. Do you sometimes find yourself fighting a losing battle against frustration, anger and helplessness? If so, here's a thought: Chill. Breathe in, breathe out. Step back. That's not to say that some things aren't sucky or rotten or awful. But it does mean that sucky and rotten and awful isn't all there is. Carpe diem; seize the day. Or better yet—go beyond seizing the day and seize the moment.

Corny but true: This moment is the only moment that you have. Tomorrow is not promised, much less next year or five years down the road. And while it is right and proper to plan for the future, it is wrong and wrong-headed to overlook today. There is beauty around you today. There is love around you today. There is life around you today--your life. But if you're too busy moaning and groaning and worrying about what the future holds, you'll miss out on the most important moment in your life--right now.

When she found out that she was dying of cancer, humorist Erma Bombeck penned a reflection called "If I Had My Life to Live Over." It ends with these words: "If I had my life to live over.... there would have been more "I love you's" and more "I'm sorry's" . . . but mostly, given another shot at life, I would seize every minute ... look at it and really see it . . . and never give it back."

Today, I will seize the moment. I will seize the day.
And I will seize it now.

Persevere

The difference between a successful person and others is not a lack of strength, not a lack of knowledge, but rather in a lack of will.

-- Vince Lombardi

It is an old story, but it bears repeating.

Many years ago, a certain gentleman had a product that he wanted to sell. His product was not unique by any means; au contraire, it was a staple in virtually every American household. So the man could not market his product based on its novelty or exclusivity. In some circles, that could be considered strike number one.

Strike number two revolved around when the period in American history when this gentleman began honing his craft. After working as blacksmith's helper and an insurance salesman, a streetcar conductor and a farmhand, the gentleman then began operating a gas station for Standard Oil. A small room in front of the gas station was where the man began testing, trying, and ultimately selling his product. But this was 1930 and the country was in the midst of the Great Depression; times were tight for everyone, regardless of the merits of what you had to sell.

If timing is indeed everything, embarking on a new business at the height of a depression seemed folly, indeed.

And strike number three involved the man's age. Although the gas station and the gentleman's small business survived, neither of them had made him wealthy. The years passed. In 1955, at the age of 65, he sold his gas station. On that same day, he collected his first social security check. Reality check! Even though he had worked his whole life, after he'd paid off his debts, he was for all intents and purposes broke. And that social security check for $105 a month wasn't going to get him out of the poorhouse.

So, five years shy of his 70th birthday, this gentleman hit the road with the product that he'd honed over the decades in tow. Despite all the strikes against him, he had three things in his favor. First of all, he believed in his product. Secondly, he had nothing to lose. And finally, perhaps most importantly, he wasn't stopped by the word "no."

Truth time: How many of us would have been discouraged after the fourth, eighth, 20th door shut in our face? Despite our belief in our product or ourselves, how many of us would have thrown in the towel and given up on our dream? This gentleman didn't. He persevered. Again...he had a $105 social security check and nothing to lose. So this fellow traveled around the country and knocked on doors. Some doors were slammed in his face, but others opened.

And after a while his product, his "secret recipe" for chicken, began to catch on. More and more people wanted a piece of it. By 1960, Colonel Harland Sanders had 190 franchises and 400 franchise units in the United States and Canada. And today Kentucky Fried Chicken-- the business the Colonel began during the Great Depression in a small booth at the front of a gas station-- is an international concern spanning 80 countries and generating billions of dollars annually. This not-quite overnight success story took decades of work and reams of rejection before hitting prime time. The race is not to the swift, but to those who stay the course. And because Col. Sanders persevered, he won.

Today I will not give up on my dream.

BEEN THERE, DONE THAT, STILL DOIN' IT

Employment tips for older workers

Resume Redux for Baby Boomers

If you weren't born in the 1980s—alas, if you actually had a job in the 1980s—chances are you're a member of the Baby Boomer generation. While some Boomers have Mickey Monkeyed off into retirement (you have to be a certain age to get that one!), others are still working that 9-5... or trying to work that 9-5. Jobs are hard to come by for everyone, but they're doubly hard to latch onto for seasoned citizens. Deborah Walker, a former headhunter and current Certified Career Management Coach, tells of a not-uncommon scenario. "You may not be ready to retire, but the young recruiters you send resumes to don't seem to respond to your skills and experience," she says. "If you're experiencing symptoms of age discrimination, you should know that your resume could be the culprit, categorizing you as out of date and over the hill."

What are the signs that your resume may need resuscitation? Two signs, says Walker, are if it uses outdated technology skills or outdated industry/ occupational terminology. But another sign that points towards Geezerville is using old school resume trends or styles. "Some of the old resume rules just don't apply anymore," Walker says. She gives the following examples:

Old School: Limit your resume to one page.

New Rule: Don't sell yourself short; this is a really old idea that limits your ability to show all of your skills and expertise.

Old School: End your resume with References Available Upon Request.

New Rule: Omit that; it's assumed.

Old School: Show every job you have ever held and give each equal importance.

New Rule: The main portion of your employment history should relate to your current employment objectives. Think of your resume as a marketing piece that highlights the best parts rather than as a tell-all. "For some years, experts have recommended that your resume should go back no more than 10 years," Walker says. "Because of background checks, however, it's best to include your full employment history, placing older experience in a section title "Previous Professional Experience," in which dates of employment are optional."

Old School: One resume should handle everything.

New Rule: Fuhgeddaboudit! And in addition to tailoring your resume to various fields or industries, you'll also need to tailor the way that you save it; have a standard Word format (for printouts and e-mail attachments) and a plain text version (for online applications).

"Let your experience work for you rather than against you," Walker says. "Using these tips to update your resume can make a noticeable difference in interest from employers."

Jumpstarting Your Job Search

If you're in Job Search Mode, doing the same thing over and over again can get tired pretty quickly. At some point, you need to press the reset button. This means that while you must still do the basics—tweaking your resume, keeping your skill set up to date, networking—maybe you can approach those basics in a slightly more creative way. By doing so, you may be able to jumpstart your job search.

In a story for AOL, blogger Rhona Bronson offered several ways to rejuvenate your job search. "The goal is to constantly do something new that refreshes not only your outlook on the world," Bronson said, "but gives you a fresh look when the world looks back at you." Four of the tips that Bronson offered are:

- Create Stories. Bronson suggests creating seven stories that you can share with a prospective employer, friend, or passerby that talks about your past work experiences. Write down at least one story a day for a week, and give each story a title so that you can quickly remember them, particularly in an interview. Some examples: Team Spirit—How I proved I was a great Team player; The Time I helped my Employer Make a Difference in the Community; Customer advocate—when I started a project from scratch that helped the company reach a new type of customer. "Do you see a pattern to the stories?" Bronson asks. "They are about you, but more importantly, they are examples of how you, as an employee, helped a company improve something."

- Write Summaries. Write one summary for LinkedIn that will appear at the top of your profile before your professional experience; it's the first thing people read when they go to your profile and tells them what you want them to know about you as a person and as a professional.

- Go to Work for Yourself. "What this means is approach each day as if you're going to work. Set your alarm. Get up a set point in time, as close to when you'd get up for an actual job. Then take a shower, comb your hair, put on your game face, and get to work," Bronson says. " You could look at job listings, write a summary or do any task at hand. The point is to create a routine that lets you approach the job hunt as a full-time job and not a part-time hobby."

- Edit yourself. Stephen King advised all writers to edit themselves by 20 percent; why should you be any different? Bronson says to pull up your resume on the computer and do a word count; do the math and challenge yourself to reduce the number of words by 20 percent. Adjectives and prepositions are key candidates to cut; delete words like "the" and "and." Bullet points can be the simplest way to reduce your word count.

"It's the little things that matter both in maintaining a positive mental attitude and keeping up your energy levels so you can put your best effort forward," Bronson concludes. "You don't have to be on all the time, but you have to give yourself the tools to make your job search time efficient."

Highlighting Transferable Skills on your Resume

For argument's sake, let's say that you are an accountant but your dream is to one day work in the biological research field. Clearly, the job description of an accountant and that of research biologist are worlds apart—but if you want to make the leap from one world into the next, you've got to find and focus on the commonalities. Job experts put it another way.

"The most effective technique career changers can use in their resumes and cover letters is transferable skills, transferable skills, transferable skills," says Maureen Crawford Hentz, an expert on social networking and media recruiting. She further advises that career changers—and only career changers—have an objective on their resume. "With my clients, I refer to these objectives as transitive objectives. Transitive objectives are those that help a potential employer understand which skills/experience the applicant thinks are transferable."

For the abovementioned example, she says that the accountant applying for a research position could say, "Seeking a biology research position that will effectively maximize my 10 years of experience as a manager with budget and supervisory responsibility." A different option: "Seeking a biology research position that will effectively maximize my experience in program and personnel management."

Hentz says that another way to highlight transferable skills is through a competency-based (or functional) resume. "Categorize prior jobs and volunteer positions as competencies so that the resume reviewer or potential employer can clearly see the transferable skills and experience," Hentz says. "Similarly, I recommend that job seekers address the career change issue directly in the cover letter. It's not necessary to self-disclose your long struggle with a job you hate, but rather briefly describe: 1. what compels you toward the new field and 2. what skills you can offer that are transferable."

Advice on Changing Careers

In 2002, after a brutal corporate layoff, Kathy Caprino decided to change careers; she got a master's degree in marriage and family therapy and become a therapist. Well, it seemed like a good idea at the time. Prior to earning the degree, Caprino had done research about the field and had interviewed therapists, but she'd never taken the profession for a test drive. In other words she never actually performed the job for any length of time in order to discover what it would be like to work eight hours straight, each and every day, helping people deal with depression, rape, incest, alcoholism, suicidal tendencies and more. Only after she'd hung up her shingle did Caprino find out what the work was really like, and for her, it was absolutely not a good fit. "Truthfully, " Caprino says, "I had just wanted out of my corporate life so badly that I longed to run as far in the other direction as possible—to the healing and helping profession. To me, that meant becoming a therapist."

Caprino, whose dream ultimately became helping women build amazing happiness, success and reward in their careers—not focus on recovery—put in a few years as a therapist before once again embarking on a second career change. "The lesson," says Caprino, is to "try on the new [career] direction as deeply and thoroughly as you can, and don't be blind to what you learn when you do." Now a nationally recognized women's career and executive coach and author of *Breakdown, Breakthrough*, Caprino offers five additional pointers to those thinking about changing career. She suggests you follow these steps in sequence.

Really and truly get in touch with yourself intimately. Know your values, your non-negotiables, your priorities and your life intentions. "If you don't know yourself deeply and thoroughly, you can't build a successful and enjoyable career," Caprino says. Also look back over your life and career and connect the dots of what you've loved to do and been naturally gifted and talented at. Enlist a mentor, friend, and coaching buddy to help you understand more clearly what you are capable of.

Release thinking and behaviors that keep you stuck. Try to uncover any limiting (often subconscious) mindsets you may have about money, power, and your worth. Note if you have communication or self-confidence issues. If so, start sorting them out and working on them. Says Caprino: "Until you let go of what you're doing and thinking that keeps you stuck and small, you can't build a happy, successful career."

Create a compelling vision. This means identifying concretely what amazing success looks like for you; break it down into a vision that fits with what you believe is possible. Once that vision is in place, get to work on it.

Explore and try on the vision. As noted above in Caprino's decision to become a therapist, it's not enough to do passive research, "Google" a new direction and read about it, or just talk to people about the career you desire. You must find any way possible to get out there and actually work at the field or in the role. That is where you'll learn if it's a good fit.

Be S.M.A.R.T. about your goals and actions. "You need a three month, six month and twelve-month plan, with Specific, Measurable, Achievable, Realistic and Time-bound goals," says Caprino, adding that you also need someone in your court to hold you accountable. "Don't try this on your own. You'll fail. Get help, build a plan with milestones that you can measure, and get on the path to expanding yourself so that you are a true match with the great, rewarding career you long for. Is a successful career change possible for you? Yes, but only if you do the inner and outer work required."

Six Tips for Working With a Younger Boss

Once you land the job, chances are very good that your boss is going to be younger than you are. Get over it. You wanted the job, you needed the job, you got the job. Now, in order to keep the job, remember this: Your boss is your boss, regardless of his or her age. And your boss deserves respect. Period. But wait…there's more. Lisa Quast, author of *Secrets of a Hiring Manager Turned Career Coach: A Foolproof Guide to Getting the Job You Want. Every Time* and Kerry Hannon, AARP Jobs expert and author of *Love Your Job: The New Rules for Career Happiness* offer their additional tips for working with a younger boss.

1. Figure out how you and your new boss can best work together. Establish a positive working relationship by finding out his or her preferred method of working and communicating. "While a previous boss (older) might have wanted formal, in-person update meetings once a week, younger managers might prefer additional, more informal communication, such as emails, text messages, or instant messaging on a daily basis," Quast says. "Flex your style to meet your new manager's style and technology of choice."

2. Talk about the elephant in the room. Hannon observes that younger bosses may wonder if you'll have a tough time reporting to someone their age. "They could be concerned

that you're not willing to try new approaches, not up to snuff with technology and might lack the grit to do the job," she says. "Tell [your boss] why he or she shouldn't worry. Better yet, show it. You could forward an article to your boss that you think is cutting edge with a note that you ran across it via one of your social media platforms."

3. Don't try to "raise" your boss; he or she is not your son or daughter. "Be an employee, not a parent," says Quast. "Based on your areas of expertise, provide helpful advice to issues and topics-- but do so in a way that doesn't come across as condescending or patronizing."

4. Keep your skills current. Let your boss know if you've recently updated any software certifications or are proficient in social media; if not, Hannon suggests that you take advantage of retraining opportunities and online courses or weekend workshops that will pump up your performance.

5. Share your background and areas of expertise, and realize that your projects or priorities may change. Quast advises that you take the time to sit down with your new boss to discuss your key projects and tasks. Try to have an open conversation about expectations (mutual expectations, if possible). Remember that your work priorities might change as your manager redefines the department or group's goals and objectives.

6. Don't act old. Hannon says to pay attention to what comes out of your mouth. "Do you persistently complain about your achy back or remind folks how things were handled back in the day?" she wonders. "If so, you're the one making age an issue."

Mission: Re-Entering The Job Market

If you've been freelancing for a while and now want to transition into the corporate world, don't expect to be greeted with open arms. In many cases, corporations see freelancers as people who are either a) too lazy to get a "real" job or b) too unqualified to rate a "real" job. You don't have to be Einstein Jr. to know that neither of these options is a good look.

Yet freelancing is something that can and should be viewed as an asset—if presented in the right way. Paradigm Staffing, a company that provides PR and communications personnel for other companies and agencies nationwide, offers the following suggestions if you're a freelancer intent on going reverse rogue.

List Projects You've Worked On. Saying that you're a freelancer tells the prospective employer nothing; elaborate. Focus on the industries you've worked on to show your versatility and give examples of the projects you've worked on. If possible, make direct connections between what the prospective employer is looking for and how it relates to the projects you've worked on. This could mean you change your examples of project work frequently to customize it for each position.

Pay Attention to Your Industry from an Employee Perspective. If you've been freelancing a while, you might not know how difficult it is to get a job in your field. Spend some time finding out what's happening and where the jobs are so that you're better prepared for your job search.

Ask Your Clients for a Job. If you've made your clients happy as a freelancer, they might be of assistance if you're looking for fulltime work. Be prepared to explain why you're getting out of freelancing. Ask your clients if they're hiring, or if they might be able to refer you to another company.

Professionalize Your Portfolio. Freelancing gives you plenty of proof of your job skills, but you'll need to make sure your portfolio is set up to highlight your skills. If appropriate, create a online portfolio on your website linking samples of your work.

Network Locally.   Many freelancers never network locally, since their gigs tend to come from all over. Now's the best time to make connections in your city that will lead to a job. Find business networking groups where professionals in your field meet to talk shop. Put it out there that you're looking for a job; you might just find a referral for one!

List Your Freelance Experience as a Business. Since many employers tend to look more positively on companies than they do on freelancers, consider listing, for instance, your writing experience as ABC Writing Company, with you as (your job title) rather than simply freelancer. Doing this will help your resume come up on a future search and via online job boards and profiles.

Don't Stop Freelancing. Finding the perfect job may take a while, so don't close up shop just yet. Continue freelancing while searching for a job, which might, in turn, help you find a fulltime job. At the very least, it will help you pay the bills until your first paycheck.

Can Volunteering Pay Off?

At first blush, volunteering seems counterintuitive—especially if you're underemployed. Let's see: Giving of your time when logic shouts you should be getting a better gig. Learning a new vocation when your skill set screams for you to go with what you know. Working for free when your bank account badgers you to earn more income. Again…working for free… instead of earning more income.

Say, whaaaat?

Yet, from a moral standpoint, there's certainly another way to look at it. Dr. Martin Luther King Jr. put it this way: "Life's most persistent and urgent question is: What are you doing for others?" Helping others—through volunteerism or otherwise—is simply the right thing to do. And the wonderful thing is that when you do something for others, you often get something in return—whether it's a sense of accomplishment, a tinge of pride, or simply a deep-down feel-good moment. But possibly, the benefits can be even more. According to Julie Shifman, founder and president of Act Three, a Cincinnati-based firm that helps women get back into the workforce, volunteering can ultimately land you a paying job. In an article she wrote for Nextavenue.org, Shifman stated that this can happen because:

Volunteering can show you're staying engaged in the work world. "Employers often prefer to interview people who are employed in some capacity, so listing a volunteer position on your resume under "Current Employment" will prevent a hiring manager from thinking you're jobless," Shifman wrote. "You don't have to mention that the job is unpaid. (Of course if you are asked, never lie). A volunteer position can help you stay up to speed in a given field and make you a more compelling candidate to employers."

You improve your LinkedIn profile. Adding a volunteer position to your LinkedIn profile lets you "link" to or connect with others in your organization or in a similar field, allowing you to introduce yourself to these potential employers and offer your services. It also makes your profile seem more robust.

You acquire new skills. Diane Rehm, host of a popular NPR show, was a stay-at-home mom before becoming a volunteer producer for a Washington, D.C. public radio station. That led to a paid position as an assistant producer and eventually a spot hosting their morning show. She stayed behind the microphone for 37 years. Prior to retiring in 2016, the Peabody Award-wining Rehm had more than 2.4 million weekly listeners.

You make new contacts. Many jobs are obtained through someone you know, so expanding your network is key.

You gain an in-depth knowledge about a specific cause. This can be a big plus if you want a paying job relating to that mission. It is on-the-job training writ large.

Your self-confidence will grow. Says Shifman: "It's easy to diminish your sense of self if you haven't worked lately (or ever), but volunteering to help others less fortunate will almost certainly give you a lift and boost your self-esteem."

The Power of Choice, Pt. 2

I truly understand that there is a lesson in everything that happens to us. So I tried not to spend my time asking "Why did this happen to me?" but trying to figure out why I had chosen this. That's the answer you need. It's always a question of accepting responsibility for your choices. Anytime you look outside yourself for answers, you're looking in the wrong place.   --Oprah Winfrey

I did not choose to be fired. I did not choose to be demoted. I did not choose this lousy job. I did not choose to get sick. I did not choose to end my marriage. I did not choose for my family to turn away from me. The dream for my life did not have me choosing to be unemployed, homeless, or coming this close to losing my mind.

So what the hell is Oprah Winfrey talking about?

In short: She's talking about getting real. And making a real honest assessment about your culpability in the matter.

She's talking about looking at your situation through new eyes, eyes that uncover how you contributed—either implicitly or explicitly—to landing yourself in the predicament that you're currently in. And beyond looking at the situation through new eyes, Winfrey is talking about learning from your current plight by really and truly understanding why things went awry. After all, the statement that "those who don't learn from history are doomed to repeat it" is as true for personal history as it is for national history. And so…

You may not have chosen to be fired but you did choose to take that job in the first place; was that really the place you ought to have been? Or would another field have been a better choice? Would opening your own business have been a wiser move?

You may have not chosen to be demoted; but did you really do everything in your power to stave off the demotion? Or did you choose not to rock the boat and, in the name of having a job, accept whatever crumbs the winds of change blew your way? Much the same can be said for having a lousy job.

And you may not have chosen to be sick, but you did choose to eat, drink, smoke or ingest things that may not have been good for you. And if you decided that exercise was nothing more than an eight-letter word, your health may very well have been affected by that choice.

You get the idea. In your relationships with spouses and family members, in your financial matters or your affairs of the home or the heart or the head, the one common element is you. Everywhere you go, there you are. And in some way, shape or form, you have a big say so in how things are going in your life. If you don't like what's going on in your world, only one person can change it. And it's not Oprah Winfrey.

Today, I will look anew at the choices I've made in my life.

Answering the Knock

Learn to listen. Opportunity could be knocking at your door very softly.   --Frank Tyger

Or, in the case of an unexpected job loss, opportunity could be banging on your door louder than a bass drum. Do you hear it? It's in that off-the-cuff conversation that you had with the woman in line at the grocery store. Do you see it? It's in that college course that you always dreamed of taking but never had the time to do so. Opportunity is waiting—if you step away from your private pity party long enough to recognize that it is there.

In 1978 Bernard Marcus and Arthur Blank were fired from their executive positions at Handy Dan, a home improvement company. Later that year they form their own company. Handy Dan went out of business in 1989. Their company Home Depot is a juggernaut.

What's an 11 letter word for opportunity? Possibility. Think about it. Isn't it possible that now, in this uncomfortable and unwanted situation, lay the seeds of a brighter tomorrow?

Possibility. Isn't it possible that leaving your old job will shine light on a new path? Possibility. Isn't it possible that right now, when you are at your lowest, a breakthrough is right around the bend? You've heard the saying a million times: when one door closes, another one opens. Opportunity could be staring you dead in the face. The question is—can you recognize and receive it? Will you accept and believe it?

When opportunity knocks, are you ready to answer?

Today, I will look and listen for an unexpected opportunity.

Rebounding From Bankruptcy

The art is not in making money, but in keeping it.

--Unknown

Know this: There's a lot of money out there.

In 2012, America had 5.2 million millionaires. In 2013, the nation's GNP neared 17 trillion dollars. And in 2016, there were 540 billionaires who call America home.

Yes, there's a lot of money out there. And there are a lot of people with money. Yet having said that, the acid test of your financial life is not in how much money you've made, it's in how much money you've saved. Because when that rainy day comes—and if it hasn't rained on you yet, just wait, because chances are that it will—you're going to need something to shelter you from the storm.

While still a teenager, Pamela Ibanez decided that she didn't like having a boss, so she spent much of her adult life working under contract. At various times she was a dancer, a model, a yoga instructor—and she spent a whole lot of time on the road.

After marriage and the birth of her first child, however, Pamela knew that it was time to focus on just one thing—and she discovered real estate investing.

You remember the start of the 21st century, don't you? In the early to mid-2000s, real estate was booming and Ibanez boomed with it. She amassed a multi-million dollar portfolio with more than 30 properties. Although things seemed fine from the outside, behind closed doors Ibanez was working so hard that she rarely saw her family and she averaged only four hours of sleep a night. Something had to give… and it did. The real estate market went bust, and it took with it everything Ibanez had worked so hard to achieve.

"I got completely wiped out," Ibanez says. "I filed bankruptcy and we lost our home to the bank. My husband left to work overseas, and I took our children and moved in with my parents. My self-confidence at this point really did not exist, and I was at the lowest of lows."

When you're really low, there's only one way for you to go: Up.

Ibanez's route out of the financial valley was through a "hobby" she'd begun in her halcyon real estate days. Back then, her work as an independent consultant for Arbonne, a skin care network marketing company, was just a little somethin' somethin' that she did on the side; now it became her lifeline to the future. Ibanez delved into the company's free training programs on topics like leadership, confidence, time management, dealing with toxic people, and so on.

Her goals were to boost her self-esteem as well as her skill-set, to spend more time with her family, and, of course, to make money. In time, she did all three. "I am now at the point where I have built up a thriving international organization, and am also enjoying lots of quality family time," she says.

Let's face it: Bankruptcy isn't at the top of most of our wish lists. But should it happen to you, remember that it's not the end of the road—it's just the end of one road. In all likelihood, there is another road you can follow that will lead to financial solvency. It's just a matter of taking it.

Today I won't let a financial setback keep me back.

Take Pride

If a man is called to be a street sweeper he should sweep streets as Michelangelo painted, or as Beethoven composed music, or Shakespeare wrote poetry. He should sweep streets so well that all the hosts of heaven and earth will pause and say, 'Here lived a great street sweeper who did his job well.'   --Martin Luther King Jr.

According to a study conducted by the Center for College Affordability and Productivity, nearly half of working Americans with college degrees are in jobs they are overqualified for. The art historian who works as a receptionist. The marketing major who moonlights as a security guard. The musician who drives a cab. Cutbacks or bad karma moved your career from one track to another...and sometimes it seems like that track isn't even in the same doggone train station you used to be in. Where you are now is not where you want to be or where you intended to be, and the fall from grace hurts. The smaller paycheck hurts. The detour of the dream hurts. But note the wording here; the dream or career didn't die--it just hit a rough patch that resulted in your taking a detour.

The thing to keep in mind is that although it may take a while, detours usually get you to your destination. And along the way these detours take you through territories and places you've never been before. Not every place you go through will be good, just as not every place you go through will be bad. But every place you go through will be necessary in order for you to reach your destination. As unanticipated, as frustrating, sometimes as demeaning as it seems to be, the detour is an important part of your journey.

So how do you handle a detour? The best way you can. Being bitter, condescending or angry makes neither your trip nor your job easier--in fact, it probably makes matters worse. The detour that you're on is not so much about what you do but about who you are while you're doing it. In all things, strive to be your highest self, your best self. Be the best cashier or security guard or receptionist that the world has ever seen, while keeping your dream alive in your heart. There's a line in a spiritual that says," trouble don't last always".... and it's true. The same can be said for detours; they're simply alternate routes to your ultimate destination. Remember that what you do is not who you are--but the way you do it is a BIG reflection of who you are. And really, at the end of the day, there's nothing to it but to do it. With competence. With congeniality. With pride.

Today I will take pride in what I do
and in who I am while I'm doing it.

Innervisions

Let yourself be silently drawn by the stronger pull of what you really love.   --Rumi

Vision boards. Wish lists. One-month, one-year, five-year plans. There's nothing new about putting on paper the plan or the goal that you have for your life; the Bible puts it this way: "Write the vision and make it plain on tablets...for the vision is yet for an appointed time." (Habakkuk 2:2, NKJV).

Sounds good, right? But...there's always a but, isn't there?... but what if nobody shares your vision? And when, exactly, is the appointed time?

Steve Harvey was 10 years old when a teacher asked the class to write down what they'd like to be when they grew up. Harvey wrote that he wanted to be on television. This was written in the 1960s, when Black folk on television were few and far between. Harvey's teacher immediately put the kibosh on little Stevie's dream—claiming that it was far-fetched and he should come up with a more realistic goal.

Fortunately, Harvey's father, Jesse, had a different mindset and although Jesse toiled as a day laborer and a coal miner (he died of black lung disease in 2000), he refused to douse his youngest child's dream. After all, many mornings while he shaved, Jesse witnessed Steve talking into his toothbrush as if it were a microphone. This kid was special. Jesse instructed Steve to keep his classwork (that sheet of paper he'd written his dream on) and place it in his dresser drawer. Jesse instructed Steve to look at it often, to keep the dream alive. Steve did, and the years passed.

The vision was on paper. But when was the appointed time?

It wasn't when Steve worked as a paperboy or a grocery clerk. It wasn't when he owned a carpet cleaning business or worked for the Ford Motor Company. It wasn't when Steve was an insurance salesman or a postman.

And the appointed time sho 'nuff wasn't when Steve began pursuing stand up comedy with a passion. "One or two gigs fell through, and suddenly I was homeless," Harvey told *People* magazine. This was no temporary situation; for three years, Steve lived out of his 1976 Ford Tempo and washed up in hotel bathrooms, gas stations, or swimming pool showers. "It was disheartening," Harvey said. "A week is really the maximum you can do. This was three years! It was rock bottom. But even in my darkest days I had faith it would turn around."

Or, as that Bible verse cited above goes on to say about having a vision: "Though it tarries, wait for it, because it will surely come."

For Harvey, what he'd written down as a 10-year-old finally came to pass in 1993 when he was tapped to host *Showtime at the Apollo*. He was 36 years old. Since then, there's been no looking back.   Harvey's hosted or starred in over a dozen television shows or series and has won numerous NAACP, Daytime Emmy, and People's Choice Awards. He's appeared in movies, written best sellers and over 7 million people listen to his daily radio show. In 2017, Harvey hosted five television shows *and* his radio show ("can't leave no paycheck behind," he joked) — giving new meaning to the phrase "the hardest working man in show business." Bottom line? Don't let anyone or anything distract you from what you know you've been called to do.

"I firmly believe that each and every one of us is born with a gift--a gift that allows you to live a life of joy, peace and prosperity," Harvey says. "The challenge that we all face is to identify that gift, learn how to cultivate that gift and then use that gift to create personal success."

Maybe it starts with writing it down and making the vision clear.

Today I will write down my dream for tomorrow.

Faith Lift

Faith is not simply a patience, which passively suffers until the storm is past. Rather, it is a spirit which bears things…with blazing, serene hope. --Corizon Aquino

Sometimes the hardest thing to do is to have faith.

It's hard to hold on to hope when things are falling apart, to believe in a brighter day when all that you can see is darkness and despair. If there's doom in each car note and gloom in every light bill, it's hard to sing "I'm happy—clap along if you feel like a room without a roof—because I'm happy" and really mean it. Because the fact of the matter is that you may very well be down to your bottom dollar, and that's a scary place to be. When fear sets in and financial ruin seems to be just a mortgage payment away, it's hard to listen to some knucklehead, like myself, exhort you to hold on and hang in there, as if this were some carnival ride and not your life that we're talking about.

Yes, sometimes the hardest thing to do is to have faith.

But the Bible puts it like this: Faith is the substance of things hoped for, the evidence of things not seen.

And so this knucklehead's question to you is this: What's so bad about that? And even more to the point: What's the alternative?

Do you pitch a bitch, give up and give in to pessimism and depression? And if you decide to go that route... exactly where do you think it is going to take you? To a land where your light bill is liquidated? To a cosmos where your car note is conveniently paid? To a galaxy where your mortgage payment will mystically and magically disappear? Probably not. After the anger and sorrow, the fear and the pity party, you're still going to be in the same situation—perhaps even a little worse for wear.

So the suggestion here is to have faith.

Clichés are called clichés because they are simple statements that are often repeated. But clichés become clichés because there's an element of truth to them. And the corny, clichéd truth about your current situation is this: It's always darkest before the dawn. Trouble don't last always. A change is gonna come.

Please know that this isn't just some loosey goosey, psychobabble, happy talk here—this is something that you must fundamentally hold on to with every fiber of your being, because your sanity depends on it. It's pretty ugly right now, but in the face of your helplessness, you've got to trust that there's going to be help. In the midst of your misery, you've got to believe that things will get better.

In the throes of your hopelessness, you've got to trust and hope in a higher power, with, as Corizon Aquino suggested, a blazing, serene hope.

It's not easy.

And it's not a cliché.

But you've got to have faith.

Today I will have faith in a brighter tomorrow.

CRASH COURSE

Dealing with career speed bumps

Why You Didn't Get the Job

It has happened to me twice (so far).

The first time, I was told by the editor in chief of a national magazine that the senior editor's position I'd applied for was mine. In fact, the human resources department had already sent my benefits packet to me. All that remained was for me to have a conversation with the publisher. Just a formality, I was told. In my mind, the conversation went well… but clearly, at times my mind can be a bit muddled.

A few days later the benefits package arrived at my house.

But I didn't get the job.

I was mortified, mystified, hot, heated, and all-around pissed off. What the…? But I survived that blow to my ego and life went on.

Flash forward ten years or so. Seeking to reinvent myself, I interviewed at a company that I was already working for on a part-time basis. The job was a marketing position—a little bit out of my field of expertise, but not by much. Plus, the people in the company knew of my work ethic and liked me…or so they said. I steadily made my way up the interview chain, culminating in an hour-long conversation with the general manager of the company. We talked about the job and how I would fit into the job and, as we parted, he smiled and said that he was pretty sure that the job was mine. Note the word "pretty." Well, I'm pretty sure you can guess where I'm going with this one.

Once again, I didn't get the job.

Maturity is a wonderful thing. This time, although I was surprised and yes, more than a little bit hurt, I was also quite philosophical --even analytical—about the whole thing. What could have possibly gone wrong? Tim Tyrell Smith, creator of Tim's Strategy, (formerly an online job search and career site) offered four reasons why some of us wind up close—but with no cigar—when it comes to landing the job of our dreams.

Not ready, not right. "As a job seeker, you always want to believe that you are ready for the next job…and your confidence is a good thing," Tyrell Smith says. "But sometimes you are simply blind to the basic gap between what ideal looks like and what you look like." Ouch. Translation: Regardless of what you think or believe about your capabilities, employers usually hire the candidate with the best experience and skill to fit the job. End of story.

Not a good match. The qualities you are expected to have in the actual position should be displayed during the job interview--so a candidate for a sales position should appear convincing, not confused; someone seeking a leadership position needs to speak decisively, not demurely; a prospective kindergarten teacher should be patient, not easily provoked. If you don't exhibit the qualities during the interview that will be needed in the job—how will your prospective employer know that you have them?

Just looking for any job. Finding the right person for a job is analogous to finding that perfect pair of shoes; someone may be able to squeeze or contort her foot into the shoe, but regardless of how it looks or what she says about that wonderful shoe, the fit just wouldn't be right. And in this instance, trying to "fake it till you make it" won't fly. "Employers can tell when your head's not in it," Tyrell Smith notes. "They can tell when the job is an OK match for you but not a great match."

Not enough energy. When Tyrell Smith surveyed hiring managers about what they looked for during an interview, they replied: Energy. Not the bouncing, frenetic, in-you-face energy of a Beyoncé concert, but a subtler energy that conveys that you're pumped and psyched about getting this job. And if you are the shy, reticent type by nature…now's the time to "fake it till you make it." Says Tyrell Smith: "Low energy in the interview says even lower energy (and productivity) on the job. You simply have to come in with energy next time."

What To Do When You Don't Get the Job

So the first, second, and third interviews went well. You were on a roll and things were looking good. Your hopes soared higher than the Empire State building and then, bam—just like that, they fell to earth. The job offer went to someone else. After all that effort, after all those smiles, you're left with, zero, nada, zilch—and you're angrier than a coat manufacturer at a nudist colony. What now? Blogger and career strategist Tim Tyrell Smith offers the following insights on what to do immediately after the bottom falls out.

Stay objective – Getting on your high horse and bemoaning your plight is easy—and non-productive. If anything is to be learned from what happened to you, you've got to keep your head clear and avoid overreacting. Only by staying objective (or as objective as you can be) may you possibly discern the real reason for your missed opportunity.

Use your network – If someone referred you for that job or if one of the people who interviewed you seemed particularly approachable, perhaps you could ask for an honest assessment on how you came off. The way you are perceived may be different from the way you THINK you are perceived—and facts are better than guesses in helping you stay objective (see previous point).

Keep on keeping on—Tyrell Smith points out that once people think they have a job in the bag, they stop looking elsewhere. "They assume that an offer is imminent and stop pursuing other options. They let their job search funnel and pipeline dry up. Not only did you not get the job but you are without momentum," he says.

Avoid appearing desperate – Desperation is never a good look. And although you may very well really, really, really need a job, try to mask sending out a desperate vibe. Companies want to hire people they feel confident in and people who feel confident in themselves—so project that image. Work to reinforce your value to the hiring company and be as relevant and confident as they want you to be.

Go get more job leads – Says Tyrell Smith: "Nothing pulls you out of a job search funk better than a new lead. So go get more job leads. Get back in touch with your network. Hit a few additional networking events. And make sure you have clear job search objectives. What are you looking for?"

Psychological Barriers That May Hinder Your Job Search

Statistics have shown that 80% of getting a job is psychological.

Now if can just stop rolling your eyes and muttering "Yeah, right" for a moment, perhaps we'll get somewhere.

Naturally, the technical stuff matters—skill set, ability, adaptability into your prospective job's culture. And the not-so-technical stuff matters—important things like who you know and who knows you. But the psychological element is also key. And in what some call the 'battlefield of the mind,' entire wars have been fought and lost without ever leaving the house.

"If you are getting in your own way and can't figure it out, you are likely to keep going round in the same circle," says Dr. Bill Knaus, Ed.D., co-author of *Fearless Job Hunting*. "It's important to watch out for and to correct consistent errors." He says that some of the biggest consistent errors job seekers make include:

Procrastination. This one comes in many guises; reading 50 books on how to write a resume; thinking that tomorrow would be a good day to start your job search; having other things that need to be done right now…other than your job search (laundry, anyone?)

Perfectionism. If your cover letter isn't flawless, if your LinkedIn page has an item missing, well, what a waste of time applying for that job would be, right? Wrong!

Fear of failure. There are no jobs out there for you in your field anyway…. so why bother? You expect to fail so you quit before you begin.

Blame. If you got turned down for a job previously, one that you just knew that you were going to get, self-blame may send you crawling into your little foxhole. And guess what? There's no job in the foxhole.

While consistent errors are to be avoided, what should be applauded—and advocated—is frequency. At its core, any job search is a numbers game. And, tiresome though it may sound, the more numbers you crank out by way of resumes sent, business cards left at different establishments, and phone calls made to potential contacts and gatekeepers (people who decide who will get interviewed for a job), the more likely you are to tip the odds in your favor.

So get cracking! Dr. Knaus suggests driving around an industrial center where the parking lot is full and going inside to talk to people about job opportunities. Or making a set of cards that has your name, address, and phone number on the front and bulleted points on the back that describe your skills and what you want in the way of a job; drop a card off wherever you go. Bottom line: You need to above and beyond…again, and again, and again. Remember that it's a numbers game. But it's also a head game.

"The psychological part of a [job] search involves cutting back on negatives like procrastination and anxieties over uncertainties," Dr. Knaus says. "Building positives, such as job-search confidence and persistence, is a key to a successful search."

Avoiding Work from Home Scams

What's not to love about a job where you can work from home…wearing your flannel PJs and sipping Joe from your favorite coffee mug? Sounds like a dream, doesn't it?

Earth to dreamer: It probably is.

"There is a 54-to-1 scam ratio among "work from home" ads on the internet, and that is not counting the ones that arrive as spam in your inbox," say Chris Durst and Michael Haaren, co-founders of Staffcentrix, a training and development firm that provides virtual career training to the US Department of State and the Armed Forces. "In other words, for every 55 [opportunities] you find on the internet, 54 will either be outright scams or downright suspicious—one will be legitimate."

How can you tell the real deal from the scam artists? Some things—like, uh, you're supposed to get PAID for the work that you do—are pretty basic, but unfortunately you often don't find out that you've been stiffed until it's too late. Other signs of a con job, however, are more nuanced. Here, courtesy of the Federal Trade Commission, are some of the more common scams to avoid.

Envelope Stuffing—The ad says that for a "small" fee, you'll learn how to earn lots of money stuffing envelopes at home. But once you pay, the fee, you find out that the only way for you to make money is to lure friends/family/other gullible people into the same envelope-stuffing "opportunity." Can you say pyramid scheme?

Assembly or craftwork—This ad leads you to believe that you can make moolah by assembling crafts or other products at home. The catch is that you may have to invest hundreds of dollars for equipment or supplies—for example, a sewing or sign making machine from the company, or material to make items like aprons or plastic signs. And after you lay out all of that money and have done the work, the company doesn't pay you, supposedly because your work isn't "up to standard." As the FTC puts it: "Unfortunately, no work ever is [up to standard], and you're left with equipment and supplies—but without any income to show for it."

Rebate Processing—The ad in your e-mail says you can earn money by helping to process rebates. And the fee for training, certification, or registration is piddling compared to what you'll earn processing rebates from home. You'll be trained by a top certified work-at-home consultant, who will show you how to succeed just like she did. But the catch here is that you'll get poorly written and useless training materials, and there are no refunds to process. Few people ever see a refund.

Online Searches—Who wouldn't want to earn an extra $500 to $1000 a week—maybe even $7000 a month—by running internet searches on prominent search engines and filling out forms? What have you got to lose, except a small shipping and handling fee? Unfortunately, you can lose a lot. In this scam, the company isn't really connected with a well-known search engine and the scammers are lying to trick you into handing over your credit or debit card information. If you pay them a tiny fee online, they use your financial information to charge you recurring fees.

Medical Billing—Bastions of aging and ailing Baby Boomers are on the horizon and health needs will increase accordingly. So the ads that promise substantial full or part-time income by processing medical claims electronically seem valid. Call a toll-free number and the sales rep assures you that for the hundreds—if not thousands—of dollars you invest to launch your own medical billing business, you'll have doctors practically banging down your door to solicit your help. Not only that, the rep says that his company will be there to provide technical support. So you spend money that you don't have to purchase the software to process the claims.... only to find that there are no potential clients and little technical support. If anything, you get an out-of-date list of doctors who haven't asked for billing services—and many doctors who do need help prefer to go with a more established billing companies that isn't operating out of someone's home. The FTC says that before entering into a medical-billing arrangement, you should ask for a sizable list of previous purchasers so that you can pick and choose whom to contact for references (otherwise, you may be given the names of one or two "shills" hired to say good things.) Try to interview people in person where the business operates. Also, talk to organizations for medical claims processors or medical billing businesses and to doctors in your community about the field. It is also prudent to consult an attorney, accountant or other business advisor before you sign an agreement or make any payments up front.

Regardless of what the work-from-home gig is, the Federal Trade Commission suggests that you ask the following:

What tasks will I have to perform? (Ask the program sponsor to list every step of the job.)

Will I be paid a salary or will I be paid on commission?

What is the basis for your claims about my likely earnings? Do you survey everyone who purchased the program? What documents can you show me to prove your claims are true before I give you any money?

Who will pay me?

When will I get my first paycheck?

What is the total cost of this work-at-home program, including supplies, equipment and membership fees? What will I get for my money?

Be sure to check out the company with your local consumer protection agency, state Attorney General and the Better Business Bureau, not only where the company is located, but also where you live. These organizations can tell you whether they've gotten complaints about a particular work-at-home program. But be wary: just because there aren't complaints doesn't mean the company is legitimate. Unscrupulous companies may settle complaints, change their names or move to avoid detection. Finally, consider other people's experience by entering the company or promoter's name with the word complaints into a search engine. Read what others have to say; this way you'll have a better understanding of what you may be getting into.

Heed these final words of wisdom from the FTC:

"When it comes to business opportunities, there are no sure bets. Promises of a big income for work from home, especially when the "opportunity" involves an up-front fee or divulging your credit card information, should make you very suspicious. It doesn't matter if the ad shows up in a trusted newspaper or website — or if the people you talk to on the phone sound legitimate. The situation demands both research and skepticism."

Identifying Controllable Career Errors

Maybe the company you loved working for went out of business. Or maybe an illness in your family forced you to uproot and scrounge for employment elsewhere. Or maybe—shudder, shudder—somewhere along the way, you just blew it. Whatever the case, the job you're currently in either isn't what you want or it makes you so miserable you could just kick the cat (Easy, PETA)! You are not alone. A 2014 job satisfaction study conducted by they Society of Human Resource Development (SHRM) found that an amazing 81 percent of Americans reported overall dissatisfaction with their present employment. Counselor educator Dr. Frank Burtnett, says that dissatisfied workers may be suffering from something he's labeled Chronic Career Disorder (CCD).

"CCD is manifested in two ways: the things we "do wrong" and the things we "don't do" --which are both likely to have a significant impact on our career achievement and emotional well-being" Burtnett says. "Either can produce harmful results."

In his book *Career Errors: Straight Talk About the Steps and Missteps of Career Development*, Burtnett talks about 25 common career errors people make throughout their working life, starting with their career choice through to their retirement and all points in between. Says Burtnett: "It's important to recognize that career errors can be traced to identifiable and controllable behaviors—things you need to monitor and manage to ensure your personal career development needs are met." Here, Burtnett cites seven of the most common controllable errors we make.

You lack quality information. Or you're solidly stuck in 2003. What are you doing to keep abreast of changes in your current and future work? What signals are your antenna picking up about new careers?

You're working with inferior tools and behaviors. Burtnett wonders, "How sharp are the tools (i.e., résumé, cover letter, etc.) and strategies (i.e., job identification tactics, interview techniques, social media strategies, etc.) that you are using in the exploration, decision-making and job-seeking process?"

You fail to learn from both good and faulty decisions. A wise person recognizes that hope is not a strategy. Are you learning from prior decisions or just crossing your fingers and hoping for the best?

Your timing is atrocious. "Choosing a career and finding a job or growing in one's career should be planned events," says Burtnett. "What have you done to prepare for, transition into, move about and evaluate the career events of your life?"

You are unsuccessful at managing or controlling the career development process. This one is a biggie. If you don't want to be locked into the same position for the next decade, Burtnett advises that you need to make some moves. Check yourself to see what steps you are taking to grow and advance. Litmus test: If your job were to suddenly disappear (i.e., budget crisis, downsizing, termination, etc.), how equipped are you to recover?

You lack flexibility and adaptability. Do you possess the ability to be both proactive and reactive? Equally as important: can you summon the right behavior at the right time?

You fail to use the people positioned to help you. There are professionally trained counselors within the career services department of every college and university to aid students in the transition from college to the workplace. And post graduation, Burtnett notes that competent recruiters and staffing professionals also exist in the private and public sector, people who can help you identify, apply for and transition into and about the world of work. Have you used any of their services?

"The college degree doesn't make you immune to career mistakes," Burtnett concludes. "Errors will not disappear. Albert Einstein once said, "A person who never made a mistake never tried anything new." However, many of the errors you will make or have already made will be your best teachers. Learn from them. They will help you rid your life of chronic career disorder."

Pursuing Your Purpose

The battles that count aren't the ones for gold medals. The struggles within yourself—the invisible, inevitable battles inside all of us—that's where it's at.   --Jesse Owens

There's no one else in the world like you.

There's no one else who has your background, your talents, your disposition, your skill set, your vision. There's no one else who can bake like you do or do math like you do or drive like you do or take care of the sick like you do or draw, design, fix houses like you do—so what are you doing?

Nada.

OK, maybe that was a bit cruel.

You're probably doing next to nada. More likely, you're doing something that isn't even in the neighborhood of what you should be doing, which is causing you to feel all kinds of bad. Your paycheck stepped into the boxing ring with your purpose, and scored a technical knockout--metaphorically speaking, of course.   But who can blame you? Bottom line: The rent has got to be paid, food has got to be put on the table, baby's gotta get a new pair of shoes. Yeah, that's what's up.

But that doesn't necessarily sit well with your soul, which is why you're feeling so listless, blah, blasé. Here's a reminder about something you already know: Money is important, but it never has been and never will be the only thing that matters. Quality of life can't be confined to dollars and cents; true quality of life comes when you live in your purpose, and it is measured by the passion and pride you display in your daily walk.

Where are you walking?

How are you walking?

If your daily walk is foreign to your comfort zone, if it leads you down streets and through alleyways that you have no desire to be on, then it's time for a change.

And that change does not mean you run out tomorrow and quit your day job.

But it is imperative that you find a way to make your life work for you, and not just the people who depend on you. Which means that if you've been blessed with the gift of sewing—use it! Design and sew clothes for others, even if there is little or no money involved. Or if you love horticulture, get some dirt under your fingers and grow and study plants, even if you live in a studio apartment. Or if you're mechanically inclined and cars are your passion, take a couple of classes at the community college to augment what you already know, even if opening your own shop is a distant dream. Can owning a clothing line or botanical garden or auto shop ever become your reality? Maybe... maybe not.

But the magic in life comes from squeezing as much joy as you can out of your day—regardless of what your 9-5 may be. That joy is found by walking in your purpose. And that purpose is always found within you.

Today I will find something I love to do and I will do it.

The Way We Were

I'm happy to report that my inner child is still ageless.

--James Broughton

John Drummond was a man with a plan. By 1999, he'd worked at IBM for 22 years, and just like his father before him, Drummond envisioned putting in his 30 years, collecting his watch and his pension, and riding off into the sunset. But IBM had other plans. The company didn't care that Drummond had a wife, a new mortgage, and three babies. When the corporate axe fell that year, it destroyed the best-laid plans of hundreds of its workers. Drummond was one of them.

Fortunately, Drummond had a fall back. Several months prior to getting fired, Drummond had started an online unicycle business. Why? Why not? As a child, Drummond loved riding his unicycle, so when he noticed an unwanted midlife paunch settling around his midsection, he dusted off his childhood toy in the hopes of losing weight. It worked. At the same time, Drummond observed that the places online that catered to the needs of the unicyclist were few and far between.

So Drummond scraped up $700 to buy a business license and six unicycles, created a website, and launched Unicyle.com. He figured that the website might provide a little side income to his IBM gig. Then the bottom fell out.

Yet every end is a beginning. With Mother IBM no longer providing for their every need, the Drummonds focused their efforts on their struggling online business. And the fates smiled down on them. About six months into their new normal, when Drummond realized that Unicycle.com might actually be able to support his family long-term, he began telling friends that he'd been "fired up." And in just eight months, this fledgling business generated more income than Drummond's full time job would have.

In August 2001 Drummond brought a new 3,200 square foot office and warehouse. Oh yes…somewhere between those two events, Drummond sent a thank-you note to his former manager, telling him that being separated from IBM was the best thing that could have happened to him.

Today, Unicycle.com, which has franchises in 14 countries, is believed to be the world's largest retailer of unicycles. In 2003, the Drummonds launched another website based on another childhood hobby, Banjo.com, which serves the needs of fellow banjo players.

That business, which was sold in 2015, has become a recognized leader in the bluegrass music industry. But Drummond says shrinking margins and competition from big-box stores made the retail space much tougher.

For a while he thought about re-entering the job market. "But once I got to captain my own ship, I found it liberating," Drummond says. "Yes, the hours can be long, but I was able to take time off for our boys' school events or soccer games. I traded one boss at IBM for a thousand bosses (customers)—and I got the better deal." In 2016, Drummond bought a Five-Star Painting franchise and, he says, "The future has never looked brighter."

Today I will recall the hopes, dreams and loves of my childhood.

Strategic Risk Taking

Start where you are. Use what you have. Do what you can.

　　　　　　　　　　　　　　　　　　--Arthur Ashe

Jennifer Musselman had been a senior public relations executive at Nickelodean for 15 years. She had all of the trappings of success—the condo, the clothing, the corner office, and the pension plan. And she wasn't happy. "I wasn't miserable, per se, but I wasn't feeling it anymore," she says.

Face it: Haven't you been there? You've worked at a job for five, ten, fifteen years because the job is what you "do," even if you don't necessarily like doing it anymore? Yet you keep plugging away because often, the benefits seem to outweigh the risks. Benefit #1: A paycheck. Benefit#2: A paycheck. Benefit #3: A paycheck. But if you're being honest with yourself, there comes a point where even the paycheck just doesn't cut it anymore. Then what? At the age of 37, Musselman decided her 'what' would be to explore a new career…while still holding on to her day job.

"The easy thing would have been to set my sights on a similar job in the same field, but I wanted to try something new," she says. Since she'd always been interested in psychology, Musselman took a few psych courses in the evening at a local college, and discovered that she loved it. Two semesters later, she enrolled in a clinical psychology graduate program while still working fulltime. Musselman's days were long and she was often tired—but she says she never felt more alive.

So you know what's coming next: Job cuts.

Truth is, being prudent doesn't prevent reality from rearing its ugly head-- but because Musselman had been prudent, she was already well down the road towards where she wanted to be. Even so, the road was scary. "You know that feeling when you're going to break up with someone, but they beat you to it?" says Musselman of being let go. "It was like that. I was prepared [to move on] but scared nonetheless." Yet the pieces fell into place. A severance package coupled with student loans gave Musselman the finances she needed to earn her degree, and two months before receiving that degree, the non-profit agency where she was training as a psychotherapist offered her a job.

Today, in addition to being a psychotherapist with her own practice, Musselman is an author, an adjunct professor at USC's Annenberg School of Communications and Journalism, and a workplace consultant. She is also the poster girl for anyone contemplating a career change. Musselman stresses the importance of 'strategic risk-taking,' or having a well thought-out plan for your exit (including money until you secure your next job) to compensate for the risk. Then go. "Test it out," she says of your impending career. "Create an exit strategy. Learn to be okay with failure. Own your decision. And move forward."

Today I will lessen the gap between where I am
and where I want to be.

Beyond the Ice Bucket

The trouble with being in the rat race is that even if you win, you're still a rat. --Lily Tomlin

Sometimes having a job, even a job that the world perceives as being a "good job," just isn't enough. Something in the human spirit yearns for satisfaction, a sense of fulfillment. And although recognition and a paycheck are wonderful, there are times when we want and need more.

Witness the case of David Steward.

Steward's is not a household name, but in some ways, his story is a common one. Born into a large African American family, Steward experienced poverty and discrimination in his youth—circumstances that only served to strengthen his resolve. He graduated from Central Missouri State University with a degree in business and eventually landed a job as a manufacturing supervisor with an electric company, but was laid off. A couple of jobs later he found himself at Federal Express, where he excelled as a senior account executive; in 1981 he was inducted into the company's Hall of Fame.

For his achievement, Steward was awarded an ice bucket with his initials engraved on it. When he looked inside the bucket, he saw that it was empty. In his book, *Doing Business by the Good Book*, Steward described this as a defining moment in his career. Was this empty ice bucket, and all that it represented, really all he wanted out of his work life?

Uh.... No.

And even though he was married and had a mortgage, two small children and "all the trappings of success that keep you locked into a job," Steward decided to take the plunge and go into business for himself. In 1984 he bought a business that audited and reviewed freight bill charges, and in 1987 he started a sister company which was hired by Union Pacific Railroad to audit three years of freight bills for undercharges. That meant managing $15 billion of rate information for this single client. Long story short: Steward needed to build a local area network to handle that data. And he did. Three years after that he founded World Wide Technology (W.W.T.), which provided businesses with technology products, services and solutions to address their specific problems. This company got off to a less than auspicious start; although he never missed a payroll, there were times when Steward couldn't pay himself. And in 1993, when the company's debt reached $3.5 million, a collection agency repossessed Steward's car right out of the company parking lot. Wow.

But Steward persevered and the company rebounded. By 2012, W.W.T. was the largest African American industrial/service company in the nation, with 2,200 employees worldwide and revenues of over $5 billion. Not bad for a company whose genesis could be traced to an empty ice bucket.

"I can't wait to come to work each morning so I can make a difference in the lives of others," Steward wrote. "I feel sorry for people who just go through the motions at work."

Today I will determine whether there are ice buckets in my life.

Swinging for the Fences

Those curveballs are always coming. Eventually, you learn to hit some of them.   --Queen Latifah

The ball game of life is full of surprises. Just when it seems as though things are under control, or going he way you want them to go, a pitch comes along that fools you. You see it coming and perhaps you go for it, swinging wildly, but miss it. Or perhaps the pitch knocks you completely off of your feet. Either way, if you're smart, you'll stay in the batters box. Because sooner or later, something might come along that you'll connect with. And when you connect with it, you might be able to hit clear out of the park.

As a young girl growing up in Denver, Karen Quinn decided that she wanted to become a lawyer. In due time, that mission was accomplished. The law firm that Quinn worked for sent her to the SEC and Quinn eventually found herself representing a gentleman whose financial futures fund was under attack; the problem was she neither knew nor cared much about what a financial futures fund was. Quinn was so bored by it all that she once fell asleep during a courtroom proceedings.

Wisely, she took that to be a cue that she might be in the wrong profession, and voluntarily sought a different career path. Being a lawyer was strike one.

She wound up working in the marketing department of American Express, and worked her way up the corporate ladder. By her fifteenth year, Quinn had made it to the rank of Vice President--enjoying all of the accouterments and perks that accompany that position. Then came the fateful day when she was called into her boss's office to hear those dreaded words: "You're downsized." Translation:

You're history, kaput, outta here. Sizzle and ouch. Being a corporate exec was strike two.

Quinn knew that if you could provide a service or do something that no one else wanted to do, you had a potential business in the making. Quinn lived in Manhattan at the time, and was well aware of the tizzy that some well-to-do Manhattanites worked themselves into as they sought to get their children into just the "right" schools. So Quinn teamed with a friend who had tons of experience in educational counseling and formed a company that helped Manhattanites get their children into the best schools. "I learned enough to convince others (and myself) that I knew what I was doing," Quinn says. "Happily, our families fared well. More importantly, I had a ringside seat at the crazy Manhattan admissions circus." This gig lasted for two and a half years, at which time Quinn once again had had enough.

The company wasn't making enough money yet to justify two salaries, so Quinn decided to walk away. Again. Since she left that situation on her own accord--strike two, ball one.

"After leaving Smart City Kids, my husband wanted me to get a job. We really needed the money," Quinn says. " But I had always had a dream about being a writer. " Quinn realized that she'd collected a wealth of funny stories during her Smart City years, and could probably turn it into a book. She told her husband that she needed three months to finish the book, and he agreed. She finished her first draft of the book in less than three months and eventually three different publishing houses made offers on the book. Movie options to *The Ivy Chronicles* were sold, and both Catherine Zeta-Jones and Sarah Jessica Parker were mentioned as potential stars of the movie. (Apparently the movie was never made.)

In any event, Quinn has gone on to write three more novels, one non-fiction book, create a website to help parents help their kids test better, and host a radio show.

"Since losing my job, my new brilliant career has been a matter of arranging whatever pieces and possibilities came my way," Quinn observes. "It's not easy, but it's what happens to many of us after a certain age. I may not be making as much money as I made at Amex, but I'm having a lot more fun working in shorts and flip flops every day, surrounded by my animals, doing what inspires me."

Did you hear the crack? That, my friend, is what you call a home run.

Today, I will swing for the fences until I come up with a hit.

STAYING CAREER SAVVY

Working it in the work world

Six Reasons Not to Quit Your Day Job

There may be a million reasons why you want to leave your day job. Your boss sucks. Your company sucks. Your pay sucks. Your co-workers suck. It's a sucky job. The sucky job is taking you nowhere. You suck at the job (Hmmmmm). Yada, yada, yada. And taken on face value, any one of those reasons may be a valid excuse for you to make like the wind and blow or make like a banana and split. Yes, the inner you may yearn to flip the finger and scream those two powerful (and potentially career-damaging) words…but the grown-up you may need to pause. Breathe. Allow cooler heads to prevail.

Bernard Marr, an internationally recognized expert in strategy and performance management, sounds this note of caution. "When you're unhappy in your current job, it's easy to see leaving as the best option," he says. "Sometimes we make rushed decisions to quit without considering all the reasons we might want to stay, such as longer term career opportunities, benefits, the opportunities in the industry, and so on."

Here, Marr gives six reasons why you may not want say "I quit" to your employer…. at least not yet.

1.) You don't have a plan. Or savings. Or a darn good job prospect waiting in the wings. How do you spell brash impulsivity? "I-Q-U-I-T."

2.) Recruiters and employers prefer hiring people who already have jobs. "It doesn't make much sense, but data confirms that employers prefer to hire people who are still employed," Marr says. "In fact, the longer you are unemployed, the harder it is to get a new job."

3.) There are benefits to staying within the same company. Sure, the days of being awarded the fancy retirement watch are so 1950s…. but longevity—even if it's for only for three or eight years—has its perks. If you can move around within your company instead of hopscotching from one company to the next, your 401K, salary history, stock options (etc.) may be better off.

4.) Willingness to leave gives you leverage; actually leaving doesn't. You can't negotiate or barter for better conditions on the job if you're no longer on the job. 'Nuff said.

5.) The grass isn't always greener. Says Marr: "Remember that just about every job comes with plusses and minuses. A job that has better benefits might come with a longer commute, and you could be leaving one bad boss for another. Before making a rash decision, consider if there are changes you can make without leaving." Marr suggests volunteering in a different department or taking a night class that may make you eligible for an alternate position within the same company. "Trying those things first might make your current position more bearable — or set you up for success when you are ready to leave."

6.)   There's a possible resume backlash. This is particularly true if you've been at the job for less than a year; employers tend to shy away from people who appear to be professional job hoppers.

Safeguarding Your Career

Maybe you're one of the lucky ones. Frankly, you're not even sure why you are reading this. You don't mind getting up in the morning, going to the job and seeing what the day will bring. Your work life is challenging, and, for the most part, fulfilling. You are doing what you want to do, where you want to do it. By and large, you are happy. And yet…it is that "and yet," that keeps you reading the words on this page. Although all is going well in your work world right now, when you're being brutally honest with yourself you have to admit that you experience occasional moments of restlessness. And there's that small, niggling voice whispering to you from the recesses of your mind telling you that you ought to be doing…something. But you're not sure what that something is. What you know for sure is this: nothing stays the same forever. The only thing constant is change. And it's better to be the bus driver than to get hit by the bus.

So now, while you're in this pretty good situation at work, it's time to put some safeguards in place for your future. Career strategist Sherri Thomas, author of *The Bounce Back: Personal stories of Bouncing Back Higher and Faster from a Layoff, Re-org, or Career Setback*, offers the following suggestions.

Turn into a jack-of-all-trades within your organization. Become knowledgeable in several key areas so that you can float seamlessly between projects or teams. This is an excellent strategy during turbulent times if companies are cutting staffs and shutting down lines of services. Letting organizations know that you're nimble, have two or three key skillsets, and add value in a variety of ways gives you a leading edge against other professionals they may be considering promoting, or hiring.

Carve out a niche for yourself. The opposite of being a jack-of-all-trades is being an expert or the "go to" person in a specialized area. Learn everything you can through training, reading books, and mentors and then apply it to your teams and projects.

Start thinking about your next career move. If you think that you'll want to freelance or do consulting somewhere down the line, create a plan that defines financial budgets, marketing strategies and potential customers. If you might want a completely new job role, research companies that are hiring and find out what their requirements are for that type of job. Make a plan on how to fill any skillset gaps with experience or training.

Use your network. Now-- when you don't need to--is the time to network like crazy. Create a professional network that's deep and wide so that if you can't answer a question or solve a problem, you know where to go to get the answer or support you need. That's just another way of saying that you need to....

Be a resource to others. People are the jet fuel behind your career. They can promote you, hire you, or introduce you to others who could potentially hire you. The key is becoming a resource for others. Send out quick e-mails with links to books or news articles that you think may interest those in your network. Volunteer to introduce your connections to others who may help them solve a problem, offer advice, or potentially advance that person's career. A key benefit of being a key resource to others is getting career support when you need it!

Using Information to your Advantage

If real estate is about location, location, location—finding or landing your dream job may be about information, information, information. Think of information as the ever present "I"—now recognize that your source for information is also ever present, right under your nose. Family, friends, neighbors—in short, the people who are already in your world—can be a font of knowledge. Your main job is to seek that information out. To do this, you may need to let go of misconceptions, prejudices and wrong-headed thinking you may not even know you possess. In his book, *Cracking the Hidden Job Market*, Donald Asher offers these three points.

1) Assume everyone has some information that will be useful to you somehow. Asher tells the following story about leading a networking game in rural Georgia. "In the networking game, a job seeker stands up in a group and says 'Who do you know who would know anything about _____?' That day a student stood up and said 'Who do you know that would know anything about being a casting director or talent agent?' I was thinking that rural Georgia was a long way from Hollywood, when a student volunteered 'My aunt is a casting director in Santa Monica.' Boom. Just like that. Expect wild connections, because they are common."

2) Don't ask to be hired; instead, seek out information. Says Asher: "You'll get a job faster by asking for information rather than for a job. When you ask people for a job, you force them into the unhappy position of having to say no to you. No one wants to say no. It makes them uncomfortable. But everyone is happy to give you advice or information. It makes them feel good."

3) It is important to connect to people with information, whether or not they have any power. Powerful people get the shine and have the credentials, but they may know little or nothing to help you in your job search. But people with information can point you in the direction of those doing the hiring and may even have a pipeline to when particular jobs are opening up. "In general, always favor information over power," Asher says. "Janitors and mechanics and receptionists can give you the critical tip you need to find your next career opportunity."

Planning For your Next Gig

A short-term job plan is one that encompasses the next five years; a long-term plan covers possibilities that may unfold further down the road. "Think of career planning as building bridges from your current job/career to your next job/career," says Randall Hansen, Ph.D., founder and former publisher of the career developmental website, Quintessential Careers. "Without the bridge, you may easily stumble or lose your way, but with the bridge there is safety and direction."

With regards to short-term planning, Dr. Hansen advises that you do the following:

Identify your next career move. If multiple career paths are on your vision board, narrow down the choices and focus on one or two careers.

Do research and gather information on the careers that most interest you.

Pinpoint the qualifications you need to move to the next step in your career or to make the move to a new career path. Dr. Hansen states that if you're not sure, search job postings and job ads, conduct informational interviews and research job descriptions.

Compare your current profile with the qualifications in the previous bullet point. How far apart are the two profiles? If fairly well-matched, Dr. Hansen says it may be time to begin your a job-search. But if they're fairly far apart, can you realistically achieve the necessary qualifications in the short-term? If yes, proceed to the next step; if no, consider returning to the first step.

Develop a plan to get qualified. List the types of qualifications you need to enhance your standing for your next career move--such as receiving additional training, certification, or experience—and develop a timeline and action plans for achieving each type. Make sure that you set specific goals and priorities.

Long-term career planning usually involves a broader set of guidelines and preparation. "Businesses, careers, and the workplace are rapidly changing, and the skills that you have or plan for today may not be in demand years from now," Dr. Hansen says. "Long-range career planning should be more about identifying and developing core skills that employers will always value while developing your personal and career goals in broad strokes." So look at:

Core Workplace Skills. Work on your communications (verbal and written), critical and creative thinking, teamwork and team-building skills, listening, social, problem-solving, decision-making, interpersonal, project management, planning and organizing and computer/technology skills. Develop a commitment to lifelong learning. Also...

Identify Career/Employment Trends. "How can you prepare for future career changes and developments?" Dr. Hansen queries. "The best way is to stay active in short-term career planning. By regularly scanning the environment and conducting research on careers, you'll quickly become an expert on the career paths that interest you -- and you'll be better prepared for your next move."

Conducting Informational Interviews

W.C. Fields once said that "If at first you don't succeed, try, try again. Then quit. There's no use being a damn fool about it."

OK... Fields had jokes—but there's a remnant of truth to what he said. If you're in a job or career that you don't like, then it's a good idea to get out of Dodge. But before you quit, take inventory; hopefully, you know what it is that you want to do next. Even so, proceed with caution. And you need to go beyond just researching your potential career on paper to really try to get the 411. Translation: Find someone in your field of interest and conduct an informational interview.

Career advisor and resume writer Dena Bilbrew explains more.

"An informational interview is one sure way to find out if your skills and qualifications match your targeted job. You can find out about the requirements and daily tasks of the position you're interested in, plus many tips for success and insight into the future of your desired field," she says. "It can also eliminate "surprises" in your actual job interview. Moreover, informational interviews can help you develop employment leads and gain experience with interviewing."

Here are nine of Bilbrew's tips on the best ways to get and conduct informational interviews.

- Pick 10 people in your desired industry that can help you. This will take some research; LinkedIn is a great place to start. These people can be in your desired position or in management.

- Decide the best method to reach out to them. Bilbrew says that if it is someone you're already acquainted with, you can just call and request some of their time. If it's someone you met at a networking event, or through a friend, maybe a brief e-mail will suffice. To contact a complete stranger, Bilbrew suggests snail mail. "Everyone loves to receive something in the mail and since not that many people actually put a stamp on things and mail them anymore, your letter will stand out. Then you can follow up within one week with a phone call." (Incidentally, Bilbrew says that she's been successful 60% of the time she used this method with strangers.) LinkedIn is also an option.

- Explain who you are and what you want from them. Be clear. Be prepared to sell yourself and let them know who you are. BRIEFLY let them know what your goal is and how you believe insight from them can help your career. Request 15-20 minutes of face-to-face time with them; use a script to stay on point if you're making this request over the phone.

- Arrive and leave on time and be prepared with your 10 questions. Pretend this is a job interview and arrive 15 minutes beforehand; pay special attention to the person's body language and be prepared to end the conversation after 20 minutes, unless he or she indicates otherwise. Naturally, the questions you ask are up to you, but some of Bilbrew's suggestions include: a. What's a typical day like in this position? What are some of your duties? b. What personal qualities or abilities are important to be successful in this job/industry? c. How do you see jobs in this field changing in the future? What special advice would you give a person entering this field?

- Show you've done your research and flatter them. "Flatter, flatter, flatter…trust me, flattery still works!" Bilbrew says. "Most people are humbled when someone actually takes a genuine interest in them and what they do. This makes them more willing to share information."

- Ask for feedback on your resume. This a) let you know what you need to do to improve it and b) it gets your resume in front of an industry professional and perhaps they will realize you might be a good fit for an opening in their company.

- Get referrals. "Everyone knows someone else at their company or in their industry that has just as much knowledge as they do. When you ask for referrals you can say, "Is there anyone else that you know who you think I should talk to get some insight? When I contact him/her may I use your name?" Bilbrew advises. Make sure you exchange business cards before leaving.

- Follow up within 24 hours. Send a thank you letter and mention something specific that you gleaned from your conversation. "Also, end it by saying something like, 'because our meeting was so brief, I was not able to completely share my background with you. I have included by LinkedIn profile/blog/online portfolio to give you additional information about me.'"

- Do it all over again with the next contact.

How to Become Career Smart

"Being career smart is not about accepting whatever job is handed to you," says career coach Sherri Thomas, "but instead it's about finding opportunities inside that job, or elsewhere, that allow you to create a career that inspires you." Thomas is the author of *Career Smart—5 Steps to a Powerful Personal Brand*, and suggests that in order to achieve a career that fills you with purpose, meaning, and passion, you do the following:

Get into a career where you can thrive. If you aren't there now, determine what career challenges you, excites you, and flexes your professional muscle. Think about what kind of work you WANT to be doing. Identify three key ingredients you need in your career to be happy and fulfilled--such as leading teams, working on creative projects, developing new technologies, etc. Once you've defined the three key ingredients, do whatever it takes to drive your career towards that vision.

Send the "right" messages. Everything you do and say sends messages to your senior managers, clients, networking contacts and potential employers. Your words, actions, presentations, status reports, resume, and interview responses all shape the perceptions others have about you. Send a crystal clear message that focuses on the value that you consistently deliver to a company or client. Your "value" is a unique blend of your strengths, professional accomplishments, and personal characteristics such as being a good leader, risk taker, problem solver, strategic thinker, etc. All of these things combined make up your "value package" which makes you truly unique from a crowd of colleagues, business associates, and even job applicants. The key is to role model the "value" that you provide by consistently demonstrating it, living it and breathing it.

Be open to possibilities. Thomas tells of almost turning down the chance to serve on the American Marketing Association's National Council because she thought this voluntary role would cut into her personal and professional life. A wise mentor advised her to reconsider, and Thomas did. Working with the Council strengthened her leadership skills, deepened her marketing expertise, and broadened her professional network, advancing her career tenfold. And a year after she joined, Thomas was named president of the Council, which bumped her career to a totally different stratosphere.

"Be assertive and aggressively seek out new career opportunities. Give serious consideration to each and every possibility that comes your way. Never decline an opportunity without getting a fresh perspective from people in your circle whom you respect," Thomas advises. "Whether you're considering a new job, or a new assignment in your current organization, answer these questions: 'What could be the best possible benefit?' 'Could this help me learn a new skill or strengthen a current skill?'

'Could this be a stepping stone to help me achieve my ultimate career goal?'"

AFTERWORD

Even as you read these words, the work world has changed again. Some of the advice given a few pages ago may already be obsolete; some of the companies mentioned may already have dissolved.

But the core of *Work It's* message is rock solid: To the best of your ability, try to live your life on your own terms. Those terms will change, depending on what season of life you are in, and those terms won't always be to your liking. But the key to getting the most out of your work life is to make sacrifices when and where you can while holding tight and holding true to that which is most dear to you. Trust and believe that it all works out.

In the intro I talked about how my husband lost his job. The truth of the matter is that Jasper was forced into early retirement, and for a time, things were pretty shaky in our household, both psychically and financially. Because he was wounded emotionally and battered economically, at first Jasper didn't seem to want to do anything but mope. It was not the best of situations. Fortunately, we had rental property, and the income generated from there helped a bit. Eventually we were able to modify the mortgage on our primary residence—and changing those terms helped a lot. But the biggest turnaround, emotionally, was that my husband returned to his first love: music. Before we married and had kids, Jasper had played bass with various bands. Now, decades later and in retirement, he formed a new band and began gigging locally. Jasper was making far less money than he had in the past, but his stress was also far less. Our expenses were slightly less. And Jasper was doing what he loved. If you want to see my music man in action, go here: www.jasperonbass.com

Angela, the daughter that I mentioned in the intro, rebounded from her job loss by going to graduate school and earning her MBA. Her student loans were colossal, but upon graduation she landed a job as a consultant with one of the top companies in her field. Although her paycheck wasn't colossal, it wasn't too paltry, either. Angela worked hard and traveled the world—but there's a season for everything. When the never-ending suitcase toting got old, she accepted an offer from another company where her job would keep her home more often. Meanwhile, my two younger children, Jelani and Jasmine, are also winding their way through the work world. Each seems content where they are for now, but I recognize that that is truly a temporary condition. The only thing constant is change.

As for myself, I've donned a couple of different hats over the last few years. I'm part owner of a small publishing company (yes, my company published this book) and I've launched an editorial services company to help individuals and businesses say what they want to say accurately, effectively, and economically. Long gone are the days of waking up at four in the morning for very little money; in fact, hindsight taught me that the best thing that can be said about having a small paycheck is that you don't miss it all that much when it's gone. Like Jasper, I am far from flush with cash, but there's enough to survive. And I am also much, much happier. The links to the publishing company and my websites are as follow: www.Dlitepress.com, www.niaceditorial.com, and www.joydcain.com

Well, that's about it. But before I go, I'd like to share a joke with you. It goes something like this:

At the end of a job interview, a Human Resources Officer asks a young engineer fresh out of school about his salary expectations.

The engineer replies, "In the region of $150,000 a year, depending on the benefits package."

The interviewer inquires, "Well, what would you say to a package of five weeks' vacation, 14 paid holidays, full medical and dental, company matching retirement fund to 50% of salary, and a company car leased every two years, say, a red Corvette?"

The engineer sits up straight and says, "Wow! Are you kidding?" The interviewer replies, "Yeah, but you started it."

Look, your work life will probably not end up being exactly as you planned. Roll with it. There will be good times and not so good times. Flow with it. Stay true to what you need to do in this moment in time, never forgetting that it's just that—a moment in time. This too, shall pass. And ultimately, the best way to use your time is to stay true to yourself. Follow the urgings of your heart, and wherever possible, *Work It!*

Namaste.

SOURCES

Donald Asher is an internationally acclaimed author and speaker specializing in professional development and higher education. He is a frequent guest on television and radio, and speaks at over 100 venues every year. Author of twelve books, including, *Cracking the Hidden Job Market, The Overnight Resume* and *How to Get Any Job,* his tomes are available in English, Chinese, Korean, and Portuguese. www.donaldasher.com

Paul Bernard is a highly respected executive coach with more than 20 years of experience advising executives on leadership development, staff management, strategic planning, communications, and work/life balance. His firm, Paul Bernard & Associates, provides cutting-edge executive coaching, onboarding, career management, and outplacement services to corporate, not-for-profit, and government executives. www.paulbernard.net

Dena Bilbrew has given career advice to over 3,000 people nationwide. After twice being laid off due to downsizing, Bilbrew realized the importance of transferable skills and the value of reinventing yourself. She founded DB Professional Concepts to assist unemployed and underemployed entry- and mid-level professionals gain the skills and confidence they need to have the career they desire. https://dbprofessionalconcepts.com, twitter.com/@DenaBilbrew

Joan Borysenko is a pioneer in integrative medicine and a world-renowned expert in the mind/body connection. A licensed psychologist and former instructor in medicine at the Harvard Medical School, Dr. Borysenko has authored or co-authored 14 books. She is the Founding Partner of Mind/Body Health Sciences, LLC in Boulder, Colorado and hosts a weekly internet radio show, Your Soul's Compass, for Hay House. www.joanborysenko.com, twitter.com/@jzborysenko

Rhona Bronson has spent more than 30 years in various marketing and communications positions with well-known consumer product and media brands. She was a contributing writer to AOL Jobs.

Les Brown is one of the world's most renowned motivational speakers. A highly sought-after resource in business and professional circles for Fortune 500 CEOs, small business owners, non-profit and community leaders looking to expand opportunities, Brown also conducts speaker-training seminars. He offers motivational material on his website, www.lesbrown.com, twitter.com/@LesBrown77

Jack Canfield is founder of the billion dollar book brand *Chicken Soup for the Soul* and a leading authority on peak performance and life success. Canfield offers life coaching as well as a free success strategies e-newsletter that can be subscribed to from his website, www.jackcanfield.com, twitter.com/@JackCanfield

Kathy Caprino is a nationally-recognized writer, trainer and speaker dedicated to the advancement of women in business. Founder/President of Ellia Communications, Inc., a leading career coaching and leadership training firm for professional and entrepreneurial women, Caprino is author of *Breakdown, Breakthrough: The Professional Woman's Guide to Claiming a Life of Passion, Power and Purpose.* kathycaprino.com , twitter.com/@kathycaprino

Caroline Ceniza-Levine is a career and business expert, writer, speaker and co-founder of SixFigureStart LLC. Prior to her move into coaching and training, Ceniza-Levine spent 15 years in strategy consulting, executive search and HR. She has appeared on CBS, CNN and Fox Business and is currently a contributor to Forbes.com. Her latest book is *Jump Ship: 10 Steps* *to Starting a New Career.* www.sixfigurestart.com, twitter.com/@PrescoPresco

Nancy Collamer is a speaker, career coach and author who contributes to NextAvenue.org, Forbes.com., and USNews.com Author of *Second-Act Careers: 50+ Ways to Profit from Your Passions During Semi-Retirement*, Collamer's website, www.mylifestylecareer.com helps people find fun, fulfilling, and flexible ways to profit from their passions during their semi-retirement years. twitter.com/@NancyCollamer

William Cowie spent 30 years in senior management (CFO/CEO) before retiring. He is CEO of Pneumesh Associates, a consulting firm specializing in helping medium to large corporations achieve exceptional growth by tapping into the cycles of the economy. Cowie also runs two blogs, one on investing and the other on the economy. www.bitethebulletinvesting.com, www.dropdeadmoney.com

Cherry Douglas is a UK-based professional career coach and career change consultant with nearly 30 years of experience. Author of the e-book *Are You Wearing The Right Suit To Work? Match your career to your Personality,* Douglas can be reached at www.how-to-change-careers.com

John Drummond's web-based business, Unicycle.com, flourished after he was forced to leave IBM in 1999. Drummond subsequently launched Banjo.com and he is currently the owner of a Five-Star Painting franchise.

Christine Durst and **Michael Haaren** are co-founders of Staffcentrix, a leader in the virtual-work/telework movement. Authors of *Work at Home Now: The No-nonsense Guide to Finding Your Perfect Home-based Job, Avoiding Scams, and Making a Great Living*, Durst and Haaren's Rat Race Rebellion website provides links to companies and industries offering home-based jobs and ads. www.ratracerebellion.com

James Feldman is a businessman and serial entrepreneur who has created and sold several businesses. Named one of the Top 100 Motivators of the Last 100 Years by Incentive magazine, he is author of *Shift Happens: No Money, No Job, Now What?* https://shifthappens.com/

Chris Gardner is an entrepreneur, author and philanthropist. In the 1980s he overcame homelessness to climb the financial industry ladder at Dean Witter Reynolds and then at Bear Stearns & Co. In 1987 he founded the Gardner Rich brokerage firm. Gardner's story was unveiled in his first book, *The Pursuit of Happyness*, which was later made into a movie starring

Will Smith. Gardner's second book, *Start Where You Are: Life Lessons in Getting from Where You Are to Where You Want to Be,* was published in 2009. www.chrisgardnermedia.com

Randall S. Hansen, Ph.D., is the founder of Quintessential Careers, one of the web's oldest and most comprehensive career development sites. An advocate for people who are struggling—or searching—for ways to improve their lives, Dr. Hansen also created EmpoweringSites.com, and has authored several books and e-books, including *Quint Careers Presents the Quintessential Guide to Job Interview Preparation.* www.randallshansen.com

Steve Harvey began doing stand-up comedy in the mid-1980s. He is a top-rated radio host, fashion entrepreneur, best-selling author, and popular television personality (at one point, he had six different shows on the air at the same time). The mission of his "Act Like a Success" movement is to empower people to get the most out of their lives. http://actlikeasuccess.com/

Maureen Crawford Hentz has more than 20 years of teaching people how to get jobs. A nationally-recognized career advice and recruiting expert, Hentz's expertise covers a range of career topics including new media recruiting, disabilities in the workplace, business etiquette, and GLBT issues.

Stephen Hopson is an award-winning Wall Street stockbroker turned transformational speaker. Profoundly deaf since birth, Hopson, the first deaf instrument-rated pilot in the world, is the author of the *Obstacle Illusions: Transforming Adversity into Success.* www.sjhopson.com

Nichole Hunn is author of numerous gluten-free cookbooks, her most recent being *Gluten-Free on a Shoestring: 125 Easy Recipes for Eating Well on the Cheap.* Her website is www.glutenfreeonashoestring.com

Pamela Ibenez, currently a real estate agent as well as a successful consultant for Arbonne, can be contacted on Facebook @PamelaIbanezArbonneIndependentConsultant

Susan Ireland has created an online resume and cover letter builder and authored multiple books on resume writing, cover letter writing, and job searching. One of those books, *The Complete Idiot's Guide to the Perfect Resume*, is in its 5th edition. Ireland apprenticed under the late resume writer Yana Parker (author of *The Damn Good Resume Guide*) and still manages Parker's website at www.damngood.com. Ireland's own website is www.susanireland.com

Susan P. Joyce is editor/publisher of two websites: the 13,000-member Job-Hunt.org, as well as WorkCoachCafe.com; both websites made Forbes magazine's list of Best 100 Websites for Your Career. Formerly a visiting scholar at the MIT Sloan School of Management, Joyce enjoys a large Twitter and online following. twitter.com/jobhuntorg, twitter.com/@workcoachcafe.com, www.job-hunt.org

Bill Knaus is a licensed clinical psychologist and former psychology professor, who has authored or co-authored more than 20 books including *Do It Now! Break the Procrastination Habit* and *Fearless Job Hunting: Powerful Psychological Strategies for Getting The Job You Want.*

Abby Kohut used her 18 years of experience and research in recruiting and Human Resources to write articles and blogs that inspire job seekers to stay motivated as they continue their search for their ideal job. Author of *Absolutely Abby's 101 Job Search Secrets*, Kohut's website was tabbed as one of the Top 100 Websites for Your Career by Forbes in 2013. twitter.com/@absolutely_abby, www.absolutelyabby.com

Bernard Marr is a globally recognized expert in strategy, performance management, analytics, and big data. Marr helps companies and executive teams manage, measure and improve performance. His latest books incliude *Big Data in Practice* and *Big Data*. twitter.com/@bernardmarr

John Maxwell is an internationally recognized leadership expert, speaker, coach, and author who has sold over 19 million books. Dr. Maxwell is the founder of EQUIP and the John Maxwell Company, organizations that have trained more than 5 million leaders worldwide. Three of Maxwell's books have sold over one million copies each: *The 21 Irrefutable Laws of Leadership, Developing the Leader Within You*, and *The 21 Indispensable Qualities of a Leader*. twitter.com/ @JohnCMaxwell www.JohnMaxwell.com

Jennifer Musselman is a life therapist and change and growth strategist. She is the co-author of three self-help books, including *The Hip Girl's Handbook for the Working World*. www.jennifermusselman.com

Bennett Neiman, Ph.D. is a nationally-recognized expert in team building, conflict resolution, strategic planning and human motivation. Founder and senior partner of Chrysalis Consulting, a full-service organizational effectiveness firm, Neiman is also the author of *Slay the Dragons-Free the Genie: Moving Past Negativity and Resistance to get Great Results*. www.chrysalis-consulting.com

Lisa Nichols is CEO of Motivating the Masses, a top training and development company. As a founding member of the Transformational Leadership Council, Lisa joins other personal and organizational development luminaries to co-create value and learning that help people change their lives and change the planet. The author of multiple books, her most recent title is *Abundance Now: Amplify Your Life and Achieve Prosperity Today.* twitter.com/@2motivate www.motivatingthemasses.com

Vicky Oliver is an award-winning author of books on career development. Her first book, *301 Smart Answers to Tough Interview Questions*, was a national bestseller and is now in its third U.S. printing. She gives seminars on job-hunting, networking, and business etiquette. twitter.com/@vickyoliver www.vickyoliver.com

Michelle Phan is a digital pioneer whose YouTube videos have had more than one billion views. An entrepreneur who founded the digital network FAWN (For All Women Network) and co-founded the beauty website ipsy.com, Phan is also the author of *Make Up: Your Life Guide to Beauty, style and Success— Online and Off.* twitter.com/@ MichellePhan www.michellephan.com

David E. Perry was nicknamed the "rogue recruiter" by the Wall Street Journal because of his unconventional approach to executive search. Perry is managing partner of Perry-Martel International, an executive search company, and author or co-author of ten books, including *Guerrilla Marketing for Job Hunters 3.0*. www.gm4jh.com

Cezary Pietrzak is a marketing strategist and mobile consultant. He's grown a variety of companies ranging from early-stage startups at AOL-backed tech incubator QLabs to Fortune 500 brands at Young & Rubicam. Pietrzak also co-founded Wanderfly, the travel discovery startup acquired by TripAdvisor, and led marketing for mobile engagement startup Appboy. Cezary Pietrzak@ckp www.cezary.co

Lisa Price is the founder of Carol's Daughter, which makes hair, body and skincare products with natural ingredients. Specializing in products for African-American women, Price started the company in 1993 and has enjoyed financial backing from celebrities like Will Smith, Jada Pinkett Smith, Mary J. Blige and Jay Z. Today Carol's Daughter products can be found nationwide, including in Walgreens and Target stores. twitter.com/@IAmLisaPrice www.carolsdaughter.com

Karen Quinn co-founded Smart City Kids, a New York City-based agency that helped families apply to the area's most competitive public and private schools. Quinn subsequently co-founded TestingMom.com, a website which helps parents help their children perform better on school tests. www.testingmom.com

Dan Schawbel is founder of Millennial Branding, a Gen Y research and consulting firm. A serial entrepreneur, Fortune 500 consultant, millennial TV personality and keynote speaker, Schawbel wrote *Promote Yourself: The New Rules For Career Success* and *Me 2.0: 4 Steps to Building Your Future*. Published prior to Schawbel's 30th birthday, those two books have been translated into 15 languages. twitter.com/@DanSchawbel www.danschawbel.com

Julie Shifman is an inspirational, award-winning speaker, author, and business owner. The founder and president of Act Three, an organization that helps women define their next stage of life and create their own personal action plan for living out that life, Shifman is also a certified coach and earned a certificate in Positive Psychology. Author of *Act Three: Creating the Life You Want*, Shifman has also created a documentary film featuring many of the incredible women profiled in her book. twitter.com/@actthree www.actthree.com

Tim Tyrell Smith is the creator of Tim's Strategy, a website dedicated to job search and career topics. Formerly a contributor to U.S. News and World Report, Tyrell Smith authored two career books (*30 Ideas* and *Headstrong*) before altering his own career path. Nonetheless, career and life information can still to be found on his website, www.timsstrategy.com

Laura Smith-Proulx is an award-winning resume writer who specializes in helping executives and rising leaders get jobs. www.AnExpertResume.com

David Steward is co-founder and Chairman of the Board of Worldwide Technologies Inc., the largest African American-owned company in the U.S. The forward of Steward's book, *Doing Business by the Good Book: 52 Lessons on Success Straight from the Bible,* was written by George H.W. Bush. www2.wwt.com

Stanley Tang is an entrepreneur, designer and developer. In 2007, 14-year-old Tang's book, *The Viral Marketing Blackbook* generated over five figures in sales. The following year, his *eMillions*, debuted at #1 on Amazon.com in four categories. In 2013 Tang co-founded DoorDash, a Palo Alto-based restaurant delivery service that has since expanded to over 40 cities nationwide. www.stanleytang.com

Sherri Thomas is a career strategist who helps others think differently and more proactively in their careers. Author of *The Bounce Back—Personal Stories of Bouncing Back Higher and Faster After a Layover, Re-org or Career Setback*, she can be reached at www.CareerCoaching360.com

Makaila Ulmer is the CEO and Founder of Me& The Bees Lemonade. This natural lemonade, made, of course, with honey, is distributed throughout the southern U.S. and along the east coast. https://meandthebees.com/

Gary Vaynerchuk is a co-founder and CEO of a VaynerMedia, a social media brand-consulting agency. Formerly a wine retail store owner, Vaynerchuk is an entrepreneur, video blogger (the DailyVee on YouTube), and author whose most recent books include *Jab, Jab, Right Hook: How to tell your story in A Noisy Social World* and the *#AskGaryVee* book. Twitter//@garyvee www.garyvaynerchuk.com

Joshua Waldman is an authority on leveraging social media to find employment. In 2017 he became President and CEO of Billy, an online accounting software made just for entrepreneurs. Author of *Job Searching With Social Media for Dummies* Waldman's award-winning career website,

CareerEnlightenment.com, provides a social media job-search class as well as profile-writing services. www.careerenlightenment.com

Deborah Walker is a Certified Career Management Coach whose expertise includes resume writing and career coaching. A former headhunter and corporate recruiter, Walker is a member of the National Resume Writer's Association.

RESOURCES

Although by no means exhaustive, the following websites are good places to begin your job search.

General Websites
Indeed.com

Simplyhired.com

Careerjet.com

Monster.com

Glassdoor.com

Government Website
USAjobs.gov

Niche Websites
Advertising: Talent Zoo.com

Accounting: Accountingjobstoday.com

Analytics, Big Data, Technology: iCrunchData

Arts: Artjobs.artsearch.us

Biotech/Pharmaceuticals: Medzilla.com

Construction: Constructionjobs.com

Creative, Design, Tech: Krop.com

Culinary Arts: Culintro.com

Design: Coroflot.com

Developers, Programmers, Engineers: Itjobpro.com

Digital Media: Digitalmediajobsnetwork.com

Energy: Energyfolks.com

Engineering: Engineerjobs.com

Finance, Banking and Insurance: eFinancialcareers.com

Flexible Work Schedules: FlexJobs.com

Health: Healthcarejobsite.com

Higher Education: HigherEdJobs.com

Human Resources: Jobs.shrm.org

Internships: Wayup.com

Information Technology: IT Job Pro

Logistics, Supply Chain, Transportation:
        JobsInLogistics.com

Luxury Brands, Retail Careers: Job-lux.com/job

Manufacturing: JobsInManufacturing.com

Media: Mediabistro.com

Nonprofits, social enterprise: Idealist.org

Politics: Politicaljobs.net

Programming, technology: Dice.com

Public Relations, communications, marketing:

PRSA.org/jobcenter

Retail: AllRetailJobs.com

Sales: SalesHeads.com

Science: Naturejobs.com

Sports: Workinsports.com

Security: ClearanceJobs.com

Trucking: JobsInTrucks.com

Web/Technology: Authenticjobs.com

Age-Specific Communities

For Teens

- CareerOneStop's Students and Career Advisors—Aimed at teens, this U.S. Department of Labor sponsored website helps viewers identify interests, explore careers, get work experience and find education options.

- Job Corps—A free education and training program that helps young people learn a career, earn a high school diploma or GED, and find and keep a good job. For eligible young people between 16-24 years of age, Job Corps provides the all-around skills needed to succeed in a career and in life.

For Young Adults

- USAJobs.gov --Newbie job hunters looking for a stable, 9-to-5 with healthcare benefits and a hefty retirement package could do far worse than beginning their search at USAJobs.gov—a tried-and-true job-search resource for students looking to gain a foothold in the government sector.

- CareerRookie.com—A division of CareerBuilder, this site connects students and recent graduates seeking internships, part-time jobs and entry-level positions with the nation's top employers.

- CollegeRecruiter.com –A leading job board for students searching for internships and recent grads looking for entry-level jobs.

- AfterCollege.com –Featuring 400,000 entry-level jobs and internships from over 25,000 employers, AfterCollege.com uses a patented job-matching algorithm to pair new job-seekers with opportunities that fit their degree, school, skills and interests.

- iHipo.com --Designed for applicants who seek international work experience, this site, boasting jobs and internships in nearly 100 countries, is the leading international graduate careers website.

- Internships.com--Brings students, employers and higher education institutions together in one centralized location.
- YouTern.com--Enables young talent to become highly employable by connecting them to high-impact internships and mentors

For Older Workers

- Workforce50.com—With a core mission is to find and provide job listings from employers truly interested in hiring from the over-50 community, this site also informative articles and helpful information related to job search
- SeniorJobBank.org—For more than a decade, this site has been committed to bringing together employers with qualified older job seekers. Its services encompass the full range of employment types and disciplines.
- Encore.org—Aimed at 50 year olds and up, this site offers "encore careers" – jobs that combine personal meaning, continued income and social impact. Its mission is to build a movement to tap into the skills and experience of those in midlife

and beyond to improve communities and the world.

Diverse Communities

- Blackcareernetwork.com—Pairs African-American job seekers with employers seeking to build a diverse workforce.
- Saludos.com-- Specializes in joining the Hispanic bilingual professional with companies looking for diversity in the workplace.
- Outandequal.org—Has an LGBTCareerLink, which offers tools and resources focused on LGBT inclusion in the workplace.
- DiversityJobs.com—This job search engine finds job listings from company career pages, other job boards, newspapers and associations.

Women

- WomensJobList.com-- Created to give employers a tool to promote diversity and inclusion within their workplaces, this site provides job seekers with easy access to those companies.
- Womenforhire.com—A job board, resume help and numerous workshops and resources for

women, including work from home options, are featured on this site.

Other

- CareerEnlightenment.com—Helps people leverage technology and use networking to get ahead in their careers.

- JobHunt.org—This site features Quick Guides to over 50 job search topics, written by genuine experts in their fields.

- Levo.com—Arms millennials with tools needed to develop their talent and build connections with peers, mentors and jobs.

- Careerarc.com—Makes it easier for job seekers to connect with employers through social media. Formerly called TweetMyJobs, this networking tool sends job recommendations via email, mobile or Twitter.

If you enjoyed this book buy now at www.joydcain.com

Also available on Amazon & NookPress.com

DLite Press

P.O. Box 824

Yorktown Heights, NY. 10598